CARRIE

THANKS FUR BEING
AN AMBASSADOR AND
FUR ALL YOU DO TO
MAKE OUR WORLD A
BETTER PLACE!

—BUOB

WHAT PEOPLE ARE SAYING ABOUT *SHOESTRINGS*

"In this book, Buddy Teaster brings together dozens of people to share the impact of Soles4Souls's life-changing work around the globe. These are stories about grit, purpose and honesty that offer lessons for non-profits and business leaders alike."

ELLEN DAVIS
President, National Retail Federation Foundation

"Shoestrings is a story of resiliency, opportunity, and overcoming. Through Buddy's candid retelling of what it takes to disrupt the cycle of poverty and create opportunity for all, we learn the power of Soles4Souls and social enterprise. A must read for anyone seeking to change the world through empowerment."

KILA ENGLEBROOK
CEO, Social Enterprise Alliance

"Soles4Souls isn't just about providing shoes to those in need. Its greater purpose is to stamp out poverty through its farsighted approach to lifting those stuck in cyclical poverty and empowering them through their micro-enterprise model. You will be inspired at every turn of the page."

EMILIE ANTONETTI
VP of Social Purpose & Managing Director, Brooks Brothers Golden Fleece Foundation

"What Soles4Souls does is wonderfully simple; they create opportunities to improve life's journey one step at a time. We are proud to be associated with an organization that does so much with so little."

DAVID MILLER
CEO, Minnetonka Moccasin

"Soles4Souls provides their partners full transparency in where donations are changing lives. The stories in this book highlight their ability to create a strategic vision and measurable impact to help wear out poverty around the world."

SHARON OH
Strategic Projects, Stitch Fix"

shoestrings

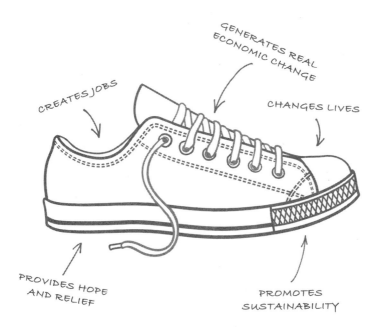

GENERATES REAL ECONOMIC CHANGE

CREATES JOBS

CHANGES LIVES

PROVIDES HOPE AND RELIEF

PROMOTES SUSTAINABILITY

shoestrings

HOW YOUR DONATED SHOES AND CLOTHES **HELP PEOPLE**
PULL THEMSELVES **OUT OF POVERTY**

BUDDY TEASTER

Published by Advantage, Charleston, South Carolina.
Member of Advantage Media Group.

ADVANTAGE is a registered trademark, and the Advantage colophon is a trademark of Advantage Media Group, Inc.

Printed in the United States of America.

10 9 8 7 6 5 4 3 2 1

ISBN: 978-1-59932-907-9
LCCN: 2018939804

Cover and layout design by Melanie Cloth.

This publication is designed to provide accurate and authoritative information in regard to the subject matter covered. It is sold with the understanding that the publisher is not engaged in rendering legal, accounting, or other professional services. If legal advice or other expert assistance is required, the services of a competent professional person should be sought.

Advantage Media Group is proud to be a part of the Tree Neutral® program. Tree Neutral offsets the number of trees consumed in the production and printing of this book by taking proactive steps such as planting trees in direct proportion to the number of trees used to print books. To learn more about Tree Neutral, please visit www.treeneutral.com.

Advantage Media Group is a publisher of business, self-improvement, and professional development books and online learning. We help entrepreneurs, business leaders, and professionals share their Stories, Passion, and Knowledge to help others Learn & Grow. Do you have a manuscript or book idea that you would like us to consider for publishing? Please visit advantagefamily.com or call 1.866.775.1696.

ABOUT THE AUTHOR

Buddy Teaster has been president and CEO of Soles4Souls since October 2012, and has since, with his amazing team, rebuilt the board and expanded partnerships and global reach all while doubling down on "disrupting the cycle of poverty." Combining entrepreneurship with his for-profit and non-profit experience, Buddy's passion for integrating business, philanthropy, and global change led him to take on the role of leading the largest social enterprise provider of shoes to those in need around the world.

From 2009 to 2012, Buddy was president and COO of StarKart. Prior to that, he was the chief network officer for the Young Presidents' Organization (YPO), a non-profit organization committed to developing better leaders through education and idea exchange. YPO is the largest CEO network in the world with more than twenty-four thousand CEOs in over one hundred countries.

His energy and enthusiasm for work spills over to his passion for running. Having run his first marathon in 1994, Buddy enjoys trail and long-distance running and has since finished more than sixty-five ultra marathons, including seventeen 100-mile runs.

Buddy earned his BA in Religious Studies and French from Randolph-Macon College in Virginia, and holds an MBA/MA from Southern Methodist University in Dallas.

He has been honored with several awards, most recently being named as one of twenty-five People Changing Retail from the National Retail Federation Foundation. He is also a Global Impact Fellow for YPO-WPO, and was named winner of YPO's 2015 Inclusive Business and Community Award.

Buddy and his wife, Becca, have been married since 1992 and have two delightful daughters.

Buddy Teaster
President & CEO, Soles4Souls
319 Martingale Dr
Old Hickory, TN 37138 USA
+1.615.391.5723
www.soles4souls.org

buddyteaster@soles4souls.org
🐦 @bteaster
in @buddyteaster

To all of those who believe that each of us has the power to make a difference—then who goes ahead and does just that.

TABLE OF CONTENTS

VII • ABOUT THE AUTHOR

XIII • FOREWORD

XVII • PREFACE AND ACKNOWLEDGMENTS

1 • INTRODUCTION
SHOESTRINGS?

PART I : BEGINNINGS

---

7 • CHAPTER 1
TSUNAMI

25 • CHAPTER 2
POVERTY: THE DAILY DISASTER

PART II: MICRO-ENTERPRISE
IN FOUR COUNTRIES

---

37 • CHAPTER 3
"WE ARE THE FORGOTTEN"— HONDURAS

53 • CHAPTER 4

A REVOLUTION CONTINUES—HAITI

69 • CHAPTER 5

"AN INVISIBLE LAND"—
TRANSNISTRIA

87 • CHAPTER 6

GOING TO AFRICA IN A BIG
WAY—SIERRA LEONE

PART III: THE PEOPLE AND VALUES
THAT ENABLE OUR WORK

---

105 • CHAPTER 7

OUR SOUL: COLLECTORS

131 • CHAPTER 8

OUR HEART: INDUSTRY PARTNERS

149 • CHAPTER 9

A NEW TWIST ON T.E.A.M.

FOREWORD

ontained in these pages is the first-hand account of the ups and downs, the highs and lows, of the Soles4Souls story—to hell and back on a shoestring. Buddy does not pull any punches as he weaves together the complex, challenging, but ultimately triumphant story that is Soles4Souls. And what a triumph it is! From the unique concept of its founder to its meteoric rise and near financial collapse to its uncompromising reemergence, this is a story that continues to be written, every single day, by the many supporters of Soles4Souls and its mission. But it all comes down to a simple, seemingly nondescript shoestring ... more on that in a minute.

From its early days of rapidly responding to natural disasters to its ongoing efforts to support micro-entrepreneurs, the story of Soles4Souls is our story. The mission of Soles4Souls is our mission. The calling of the Soles4Souls team is our calling. Scripture reminds us that "to whom much is given, much will be required," and Soles4Souls provides the outlet, the infrastructure, and the know-how to respond to this calling—one pair of shoes at a time.

And by "respond," I mean respond as an impactful community of industry partners and compassionate individuals working tirelessly to *empower* a global generation of entrepreneurs for a more hopeful and prosperous future for those in places forgotten by time and opportunity. Places like Honduras, Haiti, Sierra Leone, and

Transnistria. ("Where on Earth is Transnistria?" you might ask. You have to read on to find out!) This is where the micro-enterprise revolution is taking hold, and it is so important that you, the reader, understand this concept and its strategic importance to the success of Soles4Souls' mission of "wearing out poverty." It comes down to the small but critical difference between providing short-term relief or establishing long-lasting, sustained development as Sam Darguin of the Haitian-American Caucus (HAC) so eloquently explains in the pages of this book.

So, get ready for an exciting, educational, and very personal trip around the world, meeting and engaging with the heart and soul of this important movement—the collectors, the micro-enterprisers, the financiers, the industry partners, and the professional staff. Deepen your understanding of the importance of Soles4Souls' global networks, its micro-enterprise partners, its regional distribution centers, and the organization's passionate and self-sacrificing professional team that works daily to distribute as many shoes and clothes as possible—bringing opportunity, self-worth, and resources to those hungry to improve their lots in life.

And as you will see, this is all accomplished with an unwavering commitment to accountability and transparency so that our community's donors, supporters, and the broader footwear industry can rely on Soles4Souls' word when we commit to wearing out poverty. As a member of the Soles4Souls board of directors, I have seen first-hand Buddy's passion and unfailing commitment to organizational integrity. This passion ensures that when you do answer the call to partner with us, in ways large and small, your commitment will do exactly what it is intended to do—provide relief and equip those you have been called to serve.

But back to that shoestring. It is amazingly simple technology that serves such an important purpose to the functionality of a shoe. Shoestrings hold the shoe on your foot and bind together what we in the industry call a "functional closure." It provides connectivity and support and purpose. A shoestring is the perfect illustration of the ways in which Soles4Souls holds us all together—working as a team with our own laser-like focus on a common goal that serves a greater purpose. A shoestring is all it takes—so simple, but so vitally important to those who need us, rely on us, expect us.

So, lace up. Don't delay! Strap on your best kicks and join us on this journey to serve, empower, and love. Bring function and purpose to this worthy endeavor, because we cannot do it without you. Be a part of the sacred shoestring that binds us together, because I can assure you that Buddy, the Soles4Souls team, and the broader Soles4Souls community are just getting started.

Matt Priest
President & CEO
Footwear Distributors & Retailers of America (FDRA)

BUDDY TEASTER

PREFACE AND ACKNOWLEDGMENTS

Like most of us, I have often thought I wanted to write a book. Vaguely unsure of what it entailed, it's been on my list for a long time. This feels like the right moment to tell this story because we know where we made some good calls, where we made some mistakes, and where we just plain got lucky. But the results are there to give me enough confidence to share why it matters.

So, now it's here, and I'm amazed at both how hard and how easy it's been.

"Hard" because this story has taken a long time to play out. There were many times in the last five years when it was more likely that we would close the doors than carry on. Until just recently, the jury was out on whether the changes we had to make would really stick.

"Hard" because many of the places we work with our partners are complex, ravaged by natural disasters, uncertain regulations, low literacy, terrible infrastructure, volatile currencies, and the daily challenge of finding enough to eat.

And yet, "easy" because we are making a real dent in how people can find their own way out of poverty. You'll see some data and charts; this is a business, after all. We care about our impact and numbers help guide our decisions. But mostly you're going to hear from people who are part of a human chain that connects your closet or your warehouse or your checkbook to real people. People who are like you in many ways but in very different circumstances. We know them and soon you will, too. This is a very personal story that is full of the very personal stories of others. I hope they move you like they move me.

It's also "easy" because these stories almost tell themselves. Stories about people who stay when they could leave, who don't give up in the face of impossible odds. Stories about people who live in the tension between a brutal present and a vision of the future where their grandchildren live a life free of poverty. Stories about people who believe in the power of one person's impact and use the Soles4Souls platform to put that belief in practice.

It's been "easy" because of the amazing team who has made this book possible—the people at Advantage Media Group|Forbes Books who guided us through the publishing process; the volunteers who collect shoes and travel with us; our corporate partners all around the world; our financial supporters without whom we could not exist; a board who believes in what we're doing and holds us accountable for results; and the mind-blowingly excellent people who work at Soles4Souls to bring it all together.

In this book, I can't cover all the things that Soles4Souls does. For a small organization, we have a complicated mission that ranges from getting one pair of shoes to a homeless man in downtown Nashville to warm coats to kids on a Navajo reservation to moving hundreds of containers of shoes and clothing to dozens of countries every year. Digging deep into some of the things that I geek out on—like the Scaling Up model and Align software we use to plan and monitor our results—would bore most readers to tears. And how stunningly important apparel has become to our mission over the last few years might deserve its own book, or at least a case study. We even acquired another not-for-profit that did that!

It all matters, but it won't all fit.

There is one more "easy." That is how joyful it is to do this kind of work when I know that it's making more of a difference than anything else I've ever done. I can tell the Soles4Souls story anytime, anywhere, to anyone for the simple reason that I believe that what we do, in our small way, is the best we can do.

And that never-ending balance of "easy" and "hard" is what I get up for every morning and what drives this story.

Thanks for joining us on this journey to Wear Out Poverty.

A NOTE ABOUT THE VOICES

One goal of this book is to show Soles4Souls' impact on the full range of people involved in the organization's work: those whom benefit from it and those who make it possible. Toward that end, the in-depth perspectives of more than twenty-five people are shared here. Getting that many folks on the record is no small feat and was achieved through a joint effort.

I personally conducted interviews with those based overseas— S4S partners and beneficiaries on the ground—during business trips to their countries.

I also engaged a professional third-party interviewer, partly due to the scope of the task, but also because of the difficult subject matter around some of the organization's history. I feared that if I interviewed certain people myself—particularly those on the Soles4Souls team—my status as "the boss" might lead them to moderate their comments, and I believed a full-throated recounting of their perspectives from that period was crucial.

The material gathered in our interviews is woven into the broader work, most often in "Another Voice" features. In a few cases, the perspectives gleaned by the third-party interviewer are contextualized as conversations with me, to enhance both the narrative's readability and immediacy.

— *Buddy Teaster*
March 2018

INTRODUCTION

SHOESTRINGS?

'd like to set your mind at ease. This is *not* a book about shoe-strings. Not in the literal sense, anyway. That would be boring and I can assure you, this is anything but boring. Especially if ending poverty is important to you.

This book is about shoestrings in the *figurative* sense. As in, living on a shoestring. It's about people living in entrenched poverty and how the work of Soles4Souls, a not-for-profit social enterprise, helps them escape it.

As in, shoestring budgets. That's something Soles4Souls (S4S) knows a thing or two about because we have firsthand experience. We were living on one ourselves in 2012, when I became the organization's CEO.

In case you've never heard of us, S4S provides new and gently used shoes to people in need all over the world—with thirty million pairs distributed so far, plus literally tons of clothing.

Begun in response to the Indian Ocean tsunami that struck multiple countries in 2004, S4S was initially known as a disaster-relief organization. The catastrophe killed an estimated 230,000 to 280,000 people, and affected countless more.

When Wayne Elsey, a US-based shoe industry executive, saw a single shoe on a deserted beach as part of TV news coverage, he had a great idea: gather new shoes and send them to the survivors. His industry and other social service organizations responded in a big way: 250,000 pairs were collected and shipped to the affected areas.

The following August, Hurricane Katrina devastated New Orleans. The fledgling, still unnamed group—Soles4Souls had yet to be officially founded—acted again. This time, 750,000 pairs of shoes came in.

The story of S4S's evolution from those early efforts to the broader and deeper mission we pursue today is one of humanitarian concern, human frailty, human error, and humankind's ability to overcome seemingly insurmountable circumstances. Such challenges face the people and organizations S4S serves daily, all over the world.

Our own struggle for existence pales in comparison to theirs, but informs the work we do as a constant reminder that we've walked the same path. As shoestrings bind soles to feet, that fact keeps us tied to the people we serve, and to our mission: wearing out poverty.

PART I

BEGINNINGS

CHAPTER 1

TSUNAMI

On the day after Christmas, 2004, an estimated 230,000 to 280,000 people lost their lives when earthquake-spawned tidal waves struck fourteen countries surrounding the Indian Ocean. Among the most-fatal natural disasters of modern times, the catastrophe produced a tsunami of a different sort, weeks later: more than a quarter-million pairs of new shoes arrived in the affected countries. They'd been gathered, for free distribution to survivors, thanks to the initiative of shoe industry executive Wayne Elsey.

As Elsey recalled in his autobiography, he'd been watching TV news coverage of the tragedy. "I felt sick to my stomach. Then I saw an image of a single shoe, stranded on a decimated beach."

Elsey reached out to footwear industry colleagues and secured donations of 250,000 pairs of shoes. Working together with an array of not-for-profit organizations, they made the relief effort an unqualified success.

Less than a year later, Hurricane Katrina struck New Orleans. This time, Elsey and his colleagues collected and distributed more than 750,000 pairs of shoes.

Before long, Soles4Souls formally incorporated as a not-for-profit.

As of this writing, S4S has collected and distributed more than *thirty million* pairs of new and gently used shoes to people in need, and similarly impressive tons of clothing.

But the real story of Soles4Souls is its evolution. What started as a disaster relief organization is today a recognized pioneer of the not-for-profit social enterprise model. Today, our vision—attacking poverty in the very communities it grips most tightly—is at work around the globe.

We still distribute new shoes to people in need, at no cost. That ongoing work is a key component of our overall mission: disrupting the cycle of poverty. But it's just one facet of the work we undertake toward wider goals to serve those in need, create opportunity, and protect the environment.

Elsey's idea of collecting and distributing free shoes to those reeling from disaster made Soles4Souls' evolution to what we've become possible: an engine, providing micro-entrepreneurs with a product that is always in demand—one that can help them and their communities escape poverty's grip.

All organizations see twists and turns on their paths to success, but when Elsey resigned in 2012, Soles4Souls was facing an existential challenge the likes of which few survive. It arose through newspaper accounts of questionable business practices, dealings of which many who worked daily with Elsey were unaware.

It is therefore crucial, right here at the start, to discuss that challenge in full detail—what happened, the painstaking work we've done, and the structural changes we've made—to provide transparency in our mission, methods, and results. It's required a 180-degree shift in organizational culture, and a fundamental commitment that now guides everything we do.

But first, a little background.

HOW MUCH IS A LOT
OF SHOES?

Soles4Souls grew rapidly in its early years. Nothing illustrates that growth quite like—what else?—shoes!

A 2009 event landed the organization in the *Guinness Book of World Records:* 19,856 pairs of shoes were tied together. They stretched through a one-mile-long Nashville-area mall. Twice.

By the time I came on board—at the height (or should I say depth) of its existential crisis in mid-2012, and less than eight years after the Indian Ocean tsunami—S4S had collected and distributed more than *nineteen million* pairs of shoes worldwide. That chain would stretch from Providence, Rhode Island, to Denver, Colorado.

From mid-2012 to mid-2017, we collected eleven million *additional* pairs—extending the chain from Denver to San Francisco.

That's a lot of shoes!

Along the way, we've learned that there's a big difference between putting shoes on the feet of those who have suddenly lost everything due to natural disaster or personal calamity, and putting them on the *shelves* of micro-businesses in impoverished lands. It's the difference between, as the old adage goes, *giving* someone a fish and *teaching* them to fish.

We've seen that, by effectively orchestrating the efforts of volunteers, individual donors, not-for-profit partners on the ground, and for-profit companies, we could create a different way to solve the challenge of poverty. That together, these elements create synergies that, instead of relegating people trapped in the cycle of poverty to a day-to-day existence, allow them to build a better life for the long term.

By late 2009—just five years after the Indian Ocean tsunami, and with Elsey still at S4S's helm—the basics of this model were in place.

Then, all was nearly lost.

A SERIES OF BAD DECISIONS

After its formal incorporation in 2006, S4S began its shift toward supporting micro-enterprises in developing countries. And since we're going to be talking about micro-enterprises a lot in the chapters ahead, this is a good place to talk about what that actually means.

The worldwide reuse market for shoes and clothes is huge. ThredUP, an online retailer of secondhand apparel and footwear, estimates its global value at $18 billion, and projects it to top $33 billion by 2021. This is a big business, but not one that's been used to help people get out of poverty. Soles4Souls had stumbled on a real opportunity to change the game.

Here's how it works at S4S.

1. Repurposed shoes are donated by individuals, shoe drives, and footwear companies

2. Shoes are sent to S4S for processing and sold to vetted non-profit organizations on the ground in developing nations for an avg. of $1 per pair.

3. Our partners provide training and support where job opportunities don't exist. Selling shoes generates income individuals might not otherwise have to lift themselves out of poverty.

4. The revenue keeps Soles4Souls going! It allows us the ability to continue to give the gift of new shoes all around the world.

If Soles4Souls was going to "pivot," to use a popular Silicon Valley phrase, it did so without telling its stakeholders (the shoe donors, volunteers, and even staff who coordinated shoe drives to secure donations) how that would actually work. But a 2009 investigative report in the *Tennessean,* the paper serving S4S's hometown of Nashville, told *everyone*—describing the much-loved charity as "a middleman."

And it said far more.

Headlined, "Charity Aids Millions, Enriches Its Leader," the reporting package raised concerns about Elsey's salary and close ties to the shoe industry.

Without question, those contacts were key to the organization's highly successful responses to the Indian Ocean tsunami and Hurricane Katrina. A $20.3 million grant from the World Shoe Association, strongly pursued by Elsey, funded the organization's formal founding in 2006.

The grant did much good, securing staff positions, offices, awareness campaigns, and other infrastructure—but it *also* paid Elsey, as CEO and chairman of the board, a salary and bonus far out of line with leaders of similarly-sized charities.

The *Tennessean's* 2009 reporting noted the incongruence of not only having the charity's CEO on its board of directors but also serving as the board chair. While that's common practice in the for-profit world, it's unusual in the not-for-profit universe, as it is a potential hindrance to the board's first duty: scrutinizing the operation through independent eyes.

Sixteen months later, the *Tennessean* published another exposé. With the headline, "Shoes Charity Sells More Shoes Than It Gives Away," sitting atop of that Sunday's front page, the article led with this: "Millions of used shoes donated by churches, community groups, and individuals aren't given away for free to poor people abroad."

More than a year had passed between the investigations. Soles4Souls, and more specifically Elsey, could have spent those months educating supporters about how the organizational model had changed. The governance issues could have been addressed. The organization could have explained how its support of micro-businesses was disrupting the cycle of poverty.

Perhaps the leadership feared people would stop supporting S4S or invite still-closer scrutiny. Whatever the rationale, failure to put S4S's house in order dealt a devastating blow to the public's perception of the organization's work.

THE LAST STRAW

There's no sugar-coating what proved, for many, to be the final insult: the *Tennessean's* report that Elsey had set up and funded—with Soles4Souls' funds—a *separate* charity called Changing the World Foundation "to support" S4S. The new entity loaned Elsey $900,000 for personal real estate—a tangled arrangement later found to violate state law.

Elsey blamed the deal on bad legal advice and, with the help of S4S's then-General Counsel, undid it, ultimately freeing the organization of fiscal liability.

But it was far too little, much too late. The damage was done. Less than a year after the *Tennessean's* second investigation, Wayne Elsey resigned, and a national search for his replacement began.

STARTING FROM SCRATCH

It's difficult to overstate the role of perception in driving public opinion.

In the not-for-profit space, perception is everything. People who give time and money to causes they care about want to know—and *deserve* to know—that the people to whom they entrust these resources are good stewards.

S4S's individual donors, volunteers, and staff learned about the organization's changed approach to shoe distribution, its close ties to the shoe industry, its founder's outsized salary, and the personal loan he received not through S4S itself, but rather in their Sunday morning newspapers.

Their confidence wasn't merely shaken; it was shattered. Restoring their belief in Soles4Souls by explaining its mission and detailing how that mission was being pursued would not be an easy job. And soon, it would be mine.

Upon taking the job, I learned that Soles4Souls' fiscal picture was much worse than I or anyone else suspected—although David Graben had a pretty good idea.

ANOTHER VOICE

DAVID GRABEN
S4S CHIEF OPERATING OFFICER

"I'd been with Soles4Souls since it officially became Soles4Souls, so for me, the depth of trouble in which the organization found itself had become all too clear. Within a couple of months, Wayne Elsey resigned, the General Counsel was let go, and finally the interim CEO (who had been the COO/CFO for six years) resigned.

I was working in Haiti when a phone call came through. The board had voted me in as interim CEO and COO."

David explaining micro-enterprise in the Philippines.

"The local newspaper's investigations of Soles4Souls' board, operations, and finances pulled no punches. The fallout continued for weeks, but I didn't need a newspaper to know that something was wrong. S4S had been doing business in ways that ran counter to typical not-for-profits. That might have been okay if our supporters knew it, and if the numbers worked. Neither was the case."

"By the time Buddy was hired, many both inside and outside the organization figured it was too late to get back on track. Soles4Souls' reputation was badly tarnished. Restoring it—if that was even possible—wouldn't happen overnight."

"It's my belief that one of the board members who resigned upon Buddy's hiring wanted to bring the founder back. The other, a newer member, wanted to shut down S4S and distribute the organization's assets, and when the board voted instead to hire Buddy, he took his leave. When I imagine Buddy's reaction to that phone call—'You're hired, but … '—he must have been wondering what he was about to get himself into."

David pretty much nails it.

"The good news is we'd like to offer you the job," the board chair informed me. "The bad news is, two of our board members resigned after they voted to hire you."

The two resigning members felt just as David noted: one wanted to bring Elsey back, the other wanted to fold the tent. I don't fault either of them for their decisions. They simply didn't think a fresh start was the right direction. I also applaud them for being consistent about how to proceed; they acted according to their convictions. Nonetheless, their departures left the S4S board with just three members when I took the reins.

Today, we have a board of fifteen, with more people seeking to serve than slots available.

Getting the organization from where it was to where we are today is a story in itself. I'll share it as the book unwinds. But given what I walked into, you're probably wondering why I took the job in the first place.

COMPASSION + MARKETS = NEW SOLUTIONS

The power of combining philanthropy and markets to address poverty was and is what I love about S4S. That potential was enough for me to look past the obvious challenges and say yes. In hindsight, I didn't think I could have made things worse, and I believed I could play a role in reviving Soles4Souls.

But it was just as clear to me that success in getting Soles4Souls back on track would depend on a key commitment, embodied in one of Mark Twain's best-loved quotes: "If you tell the truth, you don't have to remember anything."

Nothing disarms and converts doubters more quickly than absolute transparency. It's a principle I was fortunate to see at work across the business world prior to joining Soles4Souls, through my involvement with the Young Presidents Organization (YPO).

A not-for-profit business leadership group, YPO works with nearly twenty thousand CEOs in 130 countries. I worked there three different times over fifteen years and learned about the value of governance, the importance of hearing all voices, and of tying all of our work back to YPO's mission: bettering leaders through education and idea exchange.

Prior to joining S4S, I switched back and forth between the not-for-profit and for-profit worlds throughout my career. But that wasn't the plan while I was in school.

My father thought I should get an education that would land me a good job. He wanted me—the first in my family to attend college—to study business and economics. So when I came home and announced that I'd be majoring in religious studies, he flipped. We "compromised," with me agreeing to also major in French. It remains the biggest argument we ever had.

I made my mother and him even crazier because then I got interested in a career in theatre. It was quickly apparent that despite being a terrible actor and a middling designer, I had some skill on the management side. It didn't look like much of a plan at the time, but following the path I found intellectually stimulating, then bouncing between the non- and for-profit worlds, proved to be perfect preparation for my work at Soles4Souls.

Well, *almost*. It turned out my parents were right. (Aren't they always?) A couple of years after earning my bachelor's, I went back to school and got an MBA and an MA in arts administration.

In more ways than one, my background is a reflection of the opportunity S4S works to give the people we serve.

The educational opportunities I received were largely due to luck: I was born in America to a family that supported me, and I was schooled within a public education system that allowed me to thrive. Helping people in poverty to build businesses and better lives for their children has proved rewarding in ways that words alone cannot adequately express. So I'll leave it at this: I love what I do at S4S more than any job I've ever had.

But there's more to the story of how I landed here.

In 2009, YPO got a new CEO—from day one, it was oil and water with us. The organizational chart is pretty clear about how that ends, and sure enough, I was quickly shown the door. So I went into business with a YPO member, Jeffrey Rosenthal, a man with whom I'd worked closely during my previous seven years at YPO. I ended up running one of his businesses, StarKart, selling ads on grocery carts.

That seems pretty disconnected from Soles4Souls, but one of his ideas was to give local businesses a connection to a charity, so the companies had something to talk about with customers. Many of the companies we served lacked the time and expertise to find relationships with suitable charities, and Soles4Souls was one we identified as a possibility.

That was pretty much all I knew of Soles4Souls until my hiring.

After I'd helped get the StarKart ship righted, it was time to either move to California, where StarKart is based, or move on. We weren't ready to leave Texas at that time, so Jeffery and I made a smooth transition. We remain great friends, and I'm happy to say that StarKart has continued to prosper and grow. They still promote Soles4Souls to their small business customers, who have collected more than ten thousand pairs of shoes since 2012!

I stood at a crossroads: I could stay in the for-profit world or re-enter the not-for-profit side, but it felt like my next turn would put me on a path for the rest of my professional life; I wasn't sure how many "bounces" were left. Thankfully, my wife, Becca, supported exploring all the options, though doing so exacted real financial and emotional costs.

Like so many things in life, the search provided clarity—and a little luck. I explored several opportunities that today I feel fortunate *not* to have taken. Then the phone rang. It was S4S's recruiter: the organization I knew of only through StarKart was looking for a new CEO. But thanks to my time at YPO, I had an amazing network I could tap into to learn more.

Surprisingly, no one in YPO was aware of the S4S job. They knew no one on the organization's board. That probably should have been more of a red flag than I allowed it to be, and I came into the interview knowing only what I could find in the paper and online. It wasn't a pretty picture, to be sure—but would it prove fatal?

NOT DEAD, BUT ON LIFE SUPPORT

Only upon reporting for work in Nashville did I learn the extreme nature of the situation.

Knowing what I know now, my best guess is that Soles4Souls' problems stemmed from a combination of the directors not asking the right questions, not having good information, and being reassured that everything was hunky-dory.

That educated guess is based on coming to understand an issue that organizations which do a lot of gift-in-kind (GIK) transactions routinely overlook: the accounting latitude they enjoy. GIK is an important concept for organizations like S4S that receive donated goods. Examples include food banks, thrift store models like Goodwill or St. Vincent de Paul, and not-for-profits that accept donated medicine or medical equipment. Organizations like ours have to assign some value to those donated goods. But, unlike for-profit businesses, where a dollar of revenue is a dollar, there are very loose guidelines about what a donated pair of shoes or a piece of furniture is worth. That means there is a lot of gray area that still allows these organizations to be in compliance with accounting and financial practices.

S4S's management team was showing gifts-in-kind as revenue. That's allowed under generally accepted accounting principles (GAAP), but the practice can mask real problems, most notably what's really happening with cash. Though legal, it's a practice that would raise concerns in the for-profit sector but often does not in the not-for-profit world—though it should be much better understood by management and directors.

That's because in-kind donations *are not cash*. You can *turn them into* cash, but when you value a pair shoes at $20 or $30 and then sell the pair for a dollar, well—it's easy to see how that could lead to bad decisions.

Another problem: S4S's mission "drift." S4S went from accepting shoes (and a little later, clothing) to taking a diverse range of items—

from wheelchairs to kitchen tile. Again, perfectly legitimate in terms of GAAP, but a veritable funhouse mirror in regard to getting a true picture of fiscal reality.

Once the board got the reins back and dug in, they began to see things were bad. But the months between the founder's departure and my arrival weren't time enough to bring the picture into sharp relief. They'd brought on an interim finance person, with an eye toward closing down the organization. It, therefore, fell to me to figure out how to keep Soles4Souls afloat.

I called on Les Ward, a friend and long-time colleague from YPO. Les is also a turnaround specialist. He knew right where to look, and his first report confirmed our worst fears: "The hole is way deeper than you thought."

Within forty-five days of my start, and without any warning, the bank pulled our overdrawn line of credit. Just like that, we were down $500,000 in cash. We were left, essentially, with nothing.

We were also in court on a couple of matters, which together had already accumulated about $1 million in legal fees. We needed to stop all that bleeding, and Les, who joined as our CFO, did a masterful job.

It took three and a half years to find a new bank. We refinanced the building. Got a new line of credit. Settled the lawsuits. We also paid everyone we owed. Some let us go for six months without paying. Some of our micro-enterprise partners in the United States paid us for products we had yet to deliver. But if we couldn't fix the business, none of that would have mattered. So that—fixing the business—became the focus.

We stopped reporting anything *except cash* to the board and to ourselves. *Each day* of those three and a half years, we faced the same question: do we have enough money to pay the bills and make payroll?

How often do you hear someone say "I'm stressed"? I'm not saying they're not stressed, but I had a different understanding of what stress means after spending a few years coming to work each morning wondering, "Is tonight when we lock this place up for the last time?"

But it went beyond that.

The frontline staff learned of S4S's problems in the newspaper, and the sense of betrayal was palpable. That's their word, not mine: *betrayal*. I'll never forget one of our team members saying, "My nana called to ask what was happening, and if we had lied to her about what we were doing." Do you know how bad and really personal things are when your grandmother calls?

I couldn't blame people for being angry, but my first priority was putting the past in the past.

"Look," I said. "I don't know everything that happened, I don't know you and you don't know me. But I can promise you this: starting right now, we're going to tell each other the truth, every day."

Which everyone thought was great. Until we started telling the truth every day! Only then did they understand: Soles4Souls was on life support.

That scared a lot of people. Some said, "Sorry, this is not for me. I need to be someplace else." Others wanted to hang in, but we had to downsize; the payroll was simply too out of whack. We went from seventy people down to thirty-five. (We're up to just over forty-five at this writing.)

THE STEPS TO RECOVERY

The departures gave us an opportunity. We could bring in people whose eyes were wide open to what they were getting into. The hiring process was completely transparent, just like everything else. We told those we wanted to hire, "You should worry." Because *we* were worried.

That might not sound like the best recruitment line, but it worked perfectly. Those who joined S4S in its darkest hours *really wanted to be there,* and I think that's why the team we have now is extraordinary.

In addition to the people who get a Soles4Souls paycheck, we've rebuilt the board. I didn't recruit any pals. We went out and got leaders from the footwear and apparel industry, from Nashville and across the country, from academia, finance, consulting, and retail. They've helped shape our strategic direction, and they hold the entire team (especially me!) accountable for results. They're doing their job by asking tough questions, and I wouldn't want it any other way.

Straightening out the governance piece not only allowed us to be better, it drove home the idea of complete transparency—internally and externally. It prompted the team to be both entrepreneurial and accountable to each other and those we serve—two of our most important values. *Each* of us helps assure that *all* of us do so.

Turning the financials around would not have happened without that transparency, without saying to everybody, "We sell shoes. That's our business model. Here's why that matters," and tying it to the mission.

The S4S tagline went from "Changing the World One Pair at a Time," which conveys and perpetuates the notion of *only* giving shoes away, to "Wearing Out Poverty," a much bigger project, prompting curiosity—and conversations—about how we make that happen. The new tagline opens the door to fully detailing the model to prospective supporters, whether they be volunteers, individual donors, or corporate partners.

Fiscally speaking, we went back to some of our corporate partners and they allowed us to continue doing cause marketing with them—a huge source of cash and awareness for us—because we said, "Here's where we are on our board, operations, and finances." We told them everything we knew and where we were headed. And most stayed with us. Without that, we could never have rebuilt.

But we did. It started with budgeting that told the real story, knowing the depth of the hole and being determined to get out of it. We didn't do anything magical. It was just executing every day, and being really clear about where we stood.

Maybe if I'd known more about what I was getting into, I'd have demurred. But I like to think not.

I was totally hooked by Soles4Souls' broader mission: the idea that social enterprise, working hand-in-hand with business, and as a business, could make real inroads to ending poverty. It just clicked, and I'm really glad it did.

I'm even happier to report that the idea is working. But how, why, and for whom?

That is what the rest of this book is about.

CHAPTER 2

POVERTY: THE DAILY DISASTER

Without question, poverty is among humankind's most pervasive challenges. The real obstacle isn't poverty itself, but something more intractable: misguided beliefs. You know the ones I mean—they assert that through hard work and determination, *anyone* can lift themselves and their family from poverty's grip.

It's just not true. It *never* was. It never will be.

There's no question that hard work and determination are crucial to achieving long-term success in any endeavor, but many of us, especially in the United States, have bought into rags-to-riches myths, which gain traction by telling just half of the story.

Of course, that's what myths do, and they have been around as long as storytelling itself. But few spread as widely or became so rooted in the American ideal as those written in the latter part of the nineteenth century by novelist Horatio Alger.

Alger's tales are formulaic to the point of predictability. Aimed at young adults, they typically feature a hardworking, impoverished adolescent boy who aspires to a middle-class life. Besides his strong work ethic, he is honest and brave—and, invariably, an act denoting one of these qualities—*not* his work ethic—catches the attention of a wealthy philanthropist. The benefactor takes the boy under his wing, paving the way for his dreamed-of ascent to the good life.

Sadly, that key ingredient in Alger's tales—*the help of others*—is often missing from today's narratives. Stories of singlehandedly rising from poverty through hard work and determination alone are a lot more impressive, after all, than those acknowledging that one had assistance.

Nonetheless, *simply being born in America* provides odds of success that people in many other countries can scarcely fathom. I talked a bit about my own luck in chapter 1, and it turns out that luck looms large when it comes to escaping poverty: both luck's presence *and* absence. Where we are born, the family we are born into, the social class we move in, and the opportunities presented to us have much to do with every individual's success.

Cornell economist Robert H. Frank, who has devoted much of his life to researching the impact of luck, puts it this way: "Successful people who believe they made it entirely on their own are almost certainly mistaken."[1]

Writing in the online magazine *Quartz*, Frank also cites the positive effects of *acknowledging* the help of others:[2]

> *[I]t's often in your interest to acknowledge luck's role in your success—if only because people will think better of you for having done so. Evidence also suggests that being grateful for your good fortune will make you feel happier.*
>
> *And by making you a more attractive potential teammate, you'll also be more likely to prosper.*

---

1   Robert H. Frank, "A Cornell Economist Who Studies Luck Says The More You Acknowledge Good Fortune, The Better Off You Are," Quartz Media LLC, (July 21, 2016): https://qz.com/733926/luck-plays-a-huge-role-in-our-success-and-admitting-it-makes-us-more-likely-to-prosper/.

2   Ibid.

Frank's research has found that an individual's chances of success—luck being a key ingredient—is enhanced by the help they get along the way, and *increases* even further when they *acknowledge* that help![3] That's the diametric opposite of the "I did it all by myself" myth, and it's why Soles4Souls tasks itself with one mission: wearing out poverty by creating *opportunity* for those not born as lucky as we are.

Soles4Souls has pursued this mission in some of the world's most impoverished lands for more than a decade, offering micro-enterprise opportunities to hardworking people in search of a better life.

Without knowing their stories, it is impossible to appreciate the challenges that people not so different from you or me awaken to on a daily basis, all over the world. This book shares those stories, and ours: how the Soles4Souls' model of social entrepreneurship is changing lives, and why we believe this model is one of human-kind's most effective tools for combating and ultimately eliminating poverty worldwide.

These stories illuminate *exactly* why hard work and determination alone do not pull people out of poverty; they need real opportunity.

UNDERSTANDING CYCLICAL POVERTY

Also called the "poverty trap," cyclical poverty transcends genera-tions. People born into poverty spend their lives struggling to make ends meet. They face hurdles to acquiring basics such as food, water, shelter, medical care, and education, to a degree most of us in the United States can scarcely comprehend. Their inability to surmount

---

3   Ibid.

those obstacles makes it impossible to escape poverty's grip. Just as children born in luckier circumstances benefit from that good fortune, the children of impoverished parents "inherit" difficult circumstances—and the cycle starts anew.

Cyclical poverty exists in every country of the world, including our own. It thrives in every conceivable setting, crippling economies at every level—from individual households to villages, to huge cities and entire countries.

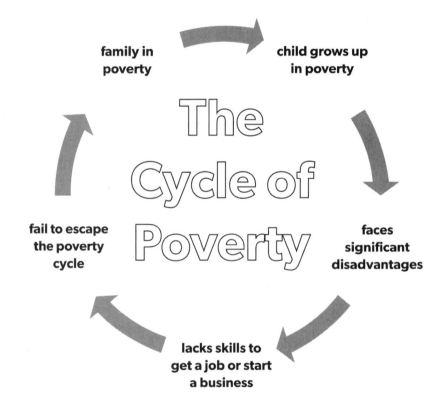

As this diagram illustrates, it is the *significant* disadvantages faced by impoverished families from generation to generation which fuel the cycle of poverty. Those disadvantages range from a lack of clean water and adequate housing to endemic disease—maladies that often find their way into the body through bare feet. They include little or no access to education and health care. They extend to a lack of jobs, or jobs that pay enough to make a difference.

Even where these essentials exist, more sinister fates can await those seeking to improve their standard of living, as we'll see when we visit Transnistria in chapter 4.

But imagine what might happen if hardworking people trapped in the cycle of poverty awakened daily not to despair, but to genuine opportunity. That "luck" is the opportunity Soles4Souls creates in countries all over the world for those we serve. The way S4S functions today—with complete transparency—is how we expect and encourage our micro-enterprise partners to operate as well. You'll meet many of them in the coming chapters.

First, let's consider an axiom at the heart of Soles4Souls' micro-enterprise model, one every entrepreneur knows is true: it takes money to make money. It's the great conundrum of capitalism. *Money* is the tool that permits people to *make* money! Through that lens, the steepness of cyclical poverty's challenge becomes clear.

That's why serious efforts to build sustainable micro-enterprises in the developing world must provide the *fundamentals* that hardworking, would-be entrepreneurs require. That means money, especially in the form of inventory: basic, always-needed consumer goods—like gently used shoes and clothing—that locally owned micro-businesses can offer their neighbors at affordable prices.

The gently used (and sometimes new) shoes and clothes Soles4Souls collects and sells to in-country distribution partners supports hardworking micro entrepreneurs who seek better lives. Some receive this inventory at no up-front cost, with payment due by the local partner only upon sale.

Our experience has shown that this model, carefully administered at every step of the process, is a sure way to disrupt the cycle of poverty. Shoes are a seed, an entry point to local economies, one that micro-businesses can cultivate, and through which they can learn the ins and outs of business firsthand.

If you're skeptical, I don't blame you. Entrenched poverty has survived all over the world for millennia. It has proved resistant to massive relief and aid efforts, created and implemented with the best of intentions.

S4S has seen this truth firsthand. We know short-term, massive relief efforts, while necessary, are not enough. Donations spawned by catastrophe eventually run out. The world's attention shifts to other issues, in other places.

But cyclical poverty remains. That truth is what prompted Soles4Souls' focus on micro-enterprise. The only certain cure for cyclical poverty is the development of sustainable local economies. Soles4Souls was fortunate in that its founding involved two men, Nelson and Paul Wilson, who realized—amid the catastrophes in the Indian Ocean and New Orleans—that donated shoes could become an engine for establishing such economies.

Their vision lives on in the work we do today: providing a consistent, reliable source of high-quality, affordable inventory to small entrepreneurs all over the world. The next four chapters tell the stories of determined women and men who are building better lives for themselves and their neighbors through micro-enterprise.

But before we meet them, there are "a couple of yahoos" you need to hear from first—similar to the Another Voice sections you've already seen where one key person's experience is highlighted, there are also Other Voices sections for multiple perspectives, as you'll see next.

OTHER VOICES

NELSON *and* PAUL WILSON

"My brother and I said back in the day that this would make a great story. How a couple of yahoos got together with someone much more sophisticated in the business world than us, and managed to ship a million pairs of shoes to people in need."

— *Nelson Wilson*

Nelson Wilson and his brother, Paul, were present at the creation of S4S, and dental work—that's right, dental work—is the reason why.

"[S4S founder] Wayne Elsey was a patient of mine," Nelson, a Nashville-area dentist, says. "I'd done a lot of mission work in South America, and I've got pictures of my different trips in different years on the walls of my office.

"Wayne had noticed those, and one day after the 2004 Indian Ocean tsunami, he just walked in my office and said, 'Hey, I'd like to send some shoes to Southeast Asia. I see this stuff on your walls. Can you contract the local churches and see if they'd collect some used shoes? I'll pay for the shipping to get them there.'"

Many months were still to pass before S4S's formal founding as a not-for-profit at this point, but thanks to their extensive humanitarian work with faith-based organizations, Nelson and Paul were perfect for the task at hand. And later—when Hurricane Katrina struck the United States—the Wilsons instantly recognized that shoes could play a key role in developing local economies.

"My brother and I started S4S's micro-enterprise ourselves. At first, Wayne had little interest. Through our work in South America, we partnered with some missionaries. We sent them some of the donated shoes that we'd stockpiled in anticipation of the next disaster, after S4S became 'official.' The missionaries got single mothers whose husbands had left them to set up little shoe shops on street corners. They would sell the used shoes for $4 or $5 a pair—and they made a living."

Nelson explained how the system worked.

"We 'fronted' them the first container of shoes, but they had to retain $1 a pair to purchase the next container. It was a business model that took care of itself, and didn't require any extra funds from Soles4Souls.

"We did it in Honduras. We did it in Guatemala. But it was under the radar, because Wayne was more focused on disaster relief and free shoe distribution. But the heart of Soles4Souls for Paul and me was micro-enterprise. We could see it becoming a huge thing. [We always] said back in the day that this would make a great story. How a couple of yahoos got together with someone much more sophisticated in the business world than us, and managed to ship a million pairs of shoes to people in need."

Nelson and Paul would become board members of S4S. Their foundational work in micro-enterprises sowed the seeds of what is now our core mission: Wearing Out Poverty. We will always be there when disaster strikes—and even when it hasn't—with new, free shoes for people in need. That is not going away, and we wouldn't want it to.

But this book looks beyond that worthy work to show S4S's micro-enterprise model in action. Until now it's been difficult do that effectively; the idea that a not-for-profit is generating revenue from its humanitarian work can't be explained in a one-page, direct-mail piece. But here, we have the time and space to do so—in depth.

The next four chapters show micro-enterprises at work in four countries. The cycle of poverty is entrenched in each, for very different reasons. And you're about to learn what impact really means in very human terms.

We begin in the first country where the Wilson brothers put Soles4Souls product to work in wearing out poverty: Honduras.

PART II

MICRO-ENTERPRISE IN FOUR COUNTRIES

CHAPTER 3

"WE ARE THE FORGOTTEN"— HONDURAS

Have you ever awakened in an unfamiliar place and wondered how you got there? Most of us have. Whether due to travel over long distances or perhaps a little too much fun on a weekend night, the disorientation that comes with waking up in strange surroundings creates intense feelings of vulnerability.

Fortunately for most of us, such experiences are momentary. We realize where we are, get our bearings (and maybe a strong cup of coffee), and go about our day. But imagine waking to and living with that intense vulnerability all day long, each and every day of your life, with little hope of things getting better.

In 2010, this was the reality for a hundred and fifty Hondurans living on the outskirts of El Progreso, a city with a population of three hundred thousand. After many years of living on the edge— literally beneath a bridge on the banks of the Ulúa River, and figuratively, since the community had no safety net—the city arbitrarily told them to leave. And if you think things couldn't get even worse, I'm sorry to say you're wrong. They did, and fast.

"We suffered a lot," Tina Martinez, one of the leaders of the displaced group, recalled. "We had to go out and find [scrap] iron to sell so we could eat."

"The city decided these people, living in hovels, were not a good image for the city. So they picked them up and moved them out into the center of a palm forest, and told them that they could live there," said Ty Hasty, of S4S partner 147 Million Orphans.

Minimal as it was, the bridge had been their home. But now they awakened daily in a strange place all over again, with no clue of how to survive—and no help from the authorities that had put them there. They were out of sight, and would be quickly forgotten.

Ty's organization was already on the ground providing relief, coordinating its efforts with the help of Sister Teresita Gonzalez, the founder of an El Progreso orphanage. One morning, she took Ty to Monte de los Olivos, the area to which the people had been forcibly relocated. Ty saw destitution at a level difficult to describe.

"They had no clean water. There was nothing to eat. And I said to Teresita, 'All these people are going to die.' She said, 'Yeah. I know.'"

Today, Olivos is a different place. Ty's organization helped residents dig wells—and build twenty-nine homes, a school, and a community center—together with Hearts2Honduras, another S4S partner.

"The biggest difference is in the people's faces," Ty said. "There's hope."

But in spite of the physical security this young community created, one question loomed: could it build an independent, sustainable future? Raul Carrasco, founder of our micro partner, World Compass Foundation, says they're "at the point of creating that opportunity."

Based in El Progreso, Raul, with Soles4Souls' help, opened a micro-enterprise in 2014, supplying shoes to micro-businesses—which, in turn, helps villagers disrupt the cycle of poverty.

"Here in Olivos, a group of women are trying to be an example," Raul tells me on a recent visit. "They are starting this project. This is a new step for them; they were not able in the past to do anything like starting a business. They weren't able to go to school. They don't have any preparation, no knowledge about how to do business, about administration.

"It's a big challenge. They are a little bit afraid about this new step. But I feel like we are working together now, and they trust each other, so they will be able to do this. It is a big, important step for them. Not everybody here understands very clearly what this group of women is doing, but I am excited, because they will be a big example for the whole community."

I asked Raul about shoes specifically; why he feels they are the right product to help bring sustainable income and growth to Olivos.

"Shoes are a big necessity," he asserts. "Look at all the kids we have here, just like any community. Every one of them needs a pair of shoes. If their family members are getting jobs by selling shoes in the marketplace, there's a collateral effect. The parents are getting jobs, and providing shoes to their kids because they are getting income.

"Money, shoes to the kids," he said, reinforcing the simple equation. "And when money is coming to the families, it's bringing other things, too. Better education, better food. It is a lot of different things. Shoes are very good and important because the demand always will be there, and growing."

I wanted to know more. Exactly how was the micro-enterprise model having a positive effect?

"First, you have to understand," Raul said, "one of the biggest problems in Honduras is that we don't have opportunities. We don't have big companies with lots of jobs here. So we are creating opportunities for the people; opportunities to generate income."

Just that succinctly, Raul made clear why I see Soles4Souls' mission as *creating luck.*

"And it's a *good* opportunity," he emphasized. "To invest in something, and start something big! We are providing the people with inexpensive, good-quality shoes, which they will be able to sell in the market with a very, very good margin of profit. It gives them the opportunity to take that profit and build up other businesses."

He shared an example.

"There's a village in the mountains where they want to optimize coffee production. They don't have the equipment that would help them do it," Raul explained. "So they are selling shoes to generate more money, to get the equipment, and become more sustainable with coffee production. It's giving people the opportunity to move up."

Just like Olivos, I thought.

ANOTHER VOICE

TIFFANY TURNER

S4S DIRECTOR OF OUTREACH/
TRAVEL COORDINATOR

"To me, Raul Carrasco is the 'Walker, Texas Ranger' of Honduras, using his powers for good, not evil—and he's capable of drop-kicking you if necessary!

I met him in August 2013, when we took our first group of volunteers to El Progreso. Raul's first involvement with Soles4Souls was primarily as a guide and translator. He worked with us in-country on our five-day trip to distribute shoes.

Tiffany Turner in Honduras.

Raul's interest in humanitarian work in his homeland began through connections with various not-for-profits based in the United States. It has literally changed his life.

I'm only half-joking about the drop-kicking, by the way: Raul is a mixed martial arts champion! He also enjoys painting, and is learning the violin. That's just the start of his many contrasting sides. Across his chest, he carries a gun and a machete (named "Mona Lisa"). But he also loves to sing a Celine Dion song, karaoke-style.

As Raul's work with Soles4Souls has evolved, so have his approaches to serving the people of his country. He runs a cross-fit gym, where he still trains and fights. Several years ago, he began taking in boys from the streets, and from bad home environments. Raul saw that the discipline of MMA offered an avenue for mentoring young men. His young NGO (non-governmental organization) in Honduras, the World Compass Foundation, trains, mentors, and develops young MMA fighters.

That word "*fighter*" perhaps sums up both Raul and what he expects of others: he fosters a fighting spirit in everyone he works with. It's why the direct micro-enterprise program he has developed with Soles4Souls is succeeding, on many levels: it benefits not only the people of villages like Olivos, but the work of Raul's foundation. It has also given him a point of focus, which is essential in a place like Honduras; the need is so great that one can be easily overwhelmed and try to do too much.

On a recent visit, Raul and I spent time with Paola, a young girl with autism, in a malnutrition center we often visit. Paola is difficult to calm down; any noise or disruption might send her into orbit.

While Raul gently rubbed her arms and hair, I sang to her, in Spanish, while Raul fed me the words. Then I stepped away and was able to take this picture—a rare moment of calm for Paola, and a window onto Raul's concern for others.

It is a privilege to work with Raul Carrasco. His commitment to his community and his country is amazing. He works hard, but remembers to stop and drink in the smallest things. Which, often, turn out to be the biggest.

Raul comforts Paolo while Tiffany sings.

EMPOWERING WOMEN

It can be tough for people in the United States to comprehend how their unused shoes, sitting in a closet, can fundamentally change lives. After all, many of us consider "ample closet space" a box to be ticked when shopping for a new home.

But, donated to S4S, those shoes change lives—every day, in countries all over the world. The ultimate beneficiaries tend to disproportionately be (and I mean this in a good way) women.

In Olivos, women tried to establish businesses that would bring sustainability to their community.

"They started working together almost from the moment of being relocated, trying to provide money to their families," Raul said. "They started a small grocery store, but that is very complicated. They were limited by what the people here were able to buy, because they don't have any money. The little market closed."

Raul introduced me to Vanessa Rodriguez, who leads the group. "Vanessa also tried to sell bracelets, things like that. But it was the same thing; it's a cyclical problem."

Vanessa said success was elusive until Raul, with the help of S4S, made it possible for the women to sell shoes. "I'm so excited that this project is finally starting, because it's an opportunity to make our own money and not have to depend on somebody else," she said.

"They have already created a plan," Raul said. "They will divide the shoes, they will go downtown and sell the shoes in the park, and around the city."

The hope in Vanessa's voice says it all: "We can really go far, because what we can make from selling the shoes that people donate is incredible. We've started selling in the marketplace. The biggest thing right now is to get the people to show up. Motivating them."

Given the failed efforts of the past, convincing people that the results will be different this time is no small feat. But Vanessa is all in.

"I've always been one of those positive people," she said. "You can't just go into something saying, 'This isn't going to work.' You've got to say, 'We're going to do this and we're going to do this well, and it's going to be a success!' The biggest focus is saving the money we bring in, because we want to form a co-op. We are saving the money instead of spending it, to find the balance between the base price of the shoe and what we get when we sell it."

Vanessa at her store in El Progreso.

That's because Raul offers the shoes to the women on credit to get them started—just as S4S does for Raul. The co-op pays Raul after the shoes are sold.

"So," Vanessa said, "we want to put the money we make into savings, and then buy a box [about five hundred pairs of shoes] ourselves, no credit. And with the profit we make from the first box, we can go back and buy two. And the next time, we can go back and buy three—maybe four."

When I asked Vanessa about their choice of business structure—why take the co-op route rather than each person fending for themselves?—she didn't miss a beat. "I'm not going to work by myself, knowing that there's a bunch of other people in the same situation. We want to make a change. We don't want to say in the end, 'Look how prosperous Vanessa is.' We want to say, 'Look how prosperous we *all* are!'"

MICRO-ENTERPRISES CAN BE EVEN SMALLER THAN YOU MIGHT THINK

The co-op that Vanessa and her associates formed is a textbook example of the fundamental change that micro-enterprises can produce.

If you're surprised by the opportunities that a few boxes of shoes can create, hold onto your hat. Small as Vanessa's group endeavor might seem, it is big in comparison to that of another fledgling entrepreneur.

Tracy Maldonado, another of Raul's customers, lives a mere twenty miles north of Olivos, but it's a world apart. Remolino, like Olivos, lies near the Ulúa River, but that's where the towns' similarities end.

Remolino is remote. Those twenty miles take more than an hour to cover. Tracy is the village leader. A cargo container of shoes would overwhelm her and the other villagers. So they're starting off with smaller quantities to better scale their efforts to the size of the market.

"We are the forgotten," Tracy said. "No government officials come here and create projects or create businesses or create opportunities for jobs. They say, 'We aren't trying to work here because other organizations are coming here and offering the opportunities.'"

"If it wasn't for us," Raul confirmed, "they would continue living as the forgotten, without any opportunity."

Tracy Maldanado sorting shoes in Remolino.

When I asked Tracy how life-changing a project like hers could be, she said, "It's very interesting how the people are responding to the project. They hear that we will have shoes and they come to my house. 'Show me the shoes, show me the shoes,' they say. They are excited because it's a good project for them. Before they started going out to sell, people were already asking about the shoes. It's a good opportunity. They are selling the shoes now, and they say that it can be very good because other people are looking at how they are working and want to get involved. The whole village, not just a group."

The differences between Olivos—which, though small itself, is adjacent a ready market of three hundred thousand people—and Remolino—with a population 959 at the last census—are stark. But the positive impacts of Tracy's micro-business are proving to be just as profound.

"If I sell one pair of shoes, it's a triple effect. I can buy medicine and some food, and I am blessing somebody with a pair of shoes at a very good price."

The effects go further. Not only is Tracy mother to four children, but she shares responsibility for eight other people in the village. In areas this remote, it's just the way things are. Tracy has other responsibilities, too. She manages a chicken farm, earning 600 *lempiras* per month, roughly $30. One dollar a day. This, along with the money she earns selling shoes, must provide for herself and the dozen other souls who count on her.

"Selling shoes here is difficult because the villagers do not have a lot of money," Tracy said. "When we go out of the village, it's good. We are thinking maybe in the future to have a store, a retail store. That's the goal."

Getting to larger markets is difficult, however. At some point, the community will have to pay for a truck to transport shoes to cities. How, Tracy admits, they don't exactly know. "It's a process," she says. "It's a process we are working on with some people I'm very close to, by talking with the local government office."

But Tracy isn't waiting until a strategy is in place. In the meantime, she's going with plan B. "There's the director of a school that is much closer [than the nearest city]. We have a good relationship with him. He has a post where he sells vegetables, and he has a car. The next step in moving out of [this] rural area is to go and put the shoes with him, so they can sell alongside the vegetables."

Different situations call for different approaches, but one constant remains: *everybody* needs a good pair of shoes. Just knowing this drives Tracy's mission. She tells me, "I'm very excited, because I will generate profit."

By empowering the women in the villages he serves, Raul is the best ambassador Soles4Souls could hope to find. His enthusiasm for his work—and for what that work will ultimately mean for his country—is infectious. I'll leave the rest of this chapter to him.

ANOTHER VOICE
RAUL CARRASCO

"'You have to dream,' I tell my customers. 'Your goal has to be big,' I say. 'It's for your families.' You have to do that, to let them know, 'You have a great opportunity here.'"

And it works.

"They get excited and say to me, 'Raul, what about if we sell these shoes, what about if we open a store in downtown?' and I say, 'That's great! That's amazing!' Because *that's* the way that I want them to think: *big*. If they do, they will show the kids, by example, that everything is different."

He shared a story of enthusiasm in action.

"Vanessa was with me in downtown, trying to get permission from the government to sell shoes there, and it was a little complicated. The process here, the bureaucracy, I think, *is* complicated—but they are not losing their motivation! They are continuing to be solid here."

Raul sees banishing negativity as a key element of his work.

"I tell them they don't have to accept any negative thing in the group. They have to talk to each other, they have to be very communicative with each other. They have to work different, you know. They will be for sure the best example of the group, the same group that was having so many problems in the past. They will be different. I think they will change the vision and the view of this village."

He admitted to his own frustration with the pace of change in Honduras, and explained how he uses it to motivate others.

Raul and Vanessa share a moment.

"We are building things here, as a country, but we are not giving opportunities to common people now to start something. Sometimes, I will talk to them about myself. I push them and I say, 'Why don't you work? Why don't you do something? Let's start something!' I'm telling them 'work,' but to start a project or start a business requires money. But right now, with the shoes and being able to start small, they have a chance, and they are excited about it."

"I asked Vanessa," he continued, "'What do you want to do if you're successful here?' and she said, 'I want to continue to study. I want to finish my studies.' That made me so happy! She already has goals.

"It's better. The lives of these people, I think, will be different because they are *thinking* differently now. That's one of the biggest problems here: changing the mentality. So I'm very thankful, because I am working with these women and they are accepting information."

To clarify this, he added: "We have to remember that some of the women never went to even one year to school. They never even went to elementary school. We have lots of challenges here, and poverty, I think sometimes, is the biggest. But I believe in these women so much because they are accepting the right information. The minds of these people are getting open, which is very good—because they will be an example to the rest of the people in the village."

Accepting information, instead of accepting the way things have always been. That's powerful.

"The potential of this project, the view of the future for these people is: kids are healthy, people are healthy. A group of women being an example to the whole community. Kids with a different future, because they will be able to go to college or have different kinds of lives, a different kind of vision.

"I've known some of these kids from when they were babies," he told me. "I've known this community [Olivos] from the beginning. I really want to see a sustainable village. I really want to see families different. I want to see healthier families, people here being able to eat better, live better, and provide a better life to their kids."

And then, Raul made something so difficult sound easy. "It's that simple, you know: better education, better health, a better future—and micro-enterprise is a big opportunity for them to get a good start. If we are able to provide them good shoes at a good price, they will be able to continue optimizing sales for better profits."

Raul's vision, I realized, is totally aligned with the S4S vision of disrupting the cycle of poverty, where generations are affected, not just for tomorrow but for years to come.

Raul is showing us the power of a great local partnership. There are things that we know about the shoe business that we share with him and his team; that's our expertise. But he knows the markets and people better than we ever can. Together, entrepreneurs, local partners, and Soles4Souls can make progress far faster than any of us could on our own. And that process started for us in Haiti, where we'll go next.

CHAPTER 4

A REVOLUTION CONTINUES—HAITI

Humanitarian work is never done in a vacuum. There's history and culture to consider. That's difficult enough when you know the place, and almost impossible when working in countries other than your own.

It's human nature to wonder about the motivations of others, particularly about those unfamiliar to us. We can see this play out right in our own neighborhoods. Who, after all, is not at least curious about the family that just moved in down the street? What brought them here? From where?

For those in some communities and countries, this basic human curiosity has been twisted into skepticism and even distrust—for sound reasons. The profound effects of European colonialism are still being felt in many of the places where S4S works, which we in the West, lacking a better vocabulary, often refer to as "developing countries."

Starting in the fifteenth century, established indigenous societies whose members lived in equilibrium with their natural environments were brutally invaded, their lands claimed by marauding outsiders from Portugal, England, Spain, and France. Those who resisted were slaughtered, and the invaders "founded" these "new" lands as their own, establishing top-down, repressive governance that enslaved local people to produce goods that enriched both the occupiers and their homelands' monarchs.

Too often, in addition to the subject territory's crops and mineral wealth, colonists exported its human capital as well, commoditizing humans—slaves—for personal and national gain.

The intervening centuries have seen indigenous peoples rising up to reclaim their lands, a struggle still playing out in places around the world, from the United States to Honduras, from Sierra Leone to Malawi.

One of the earliest successful revolts against colonialism in the Western hemisphere—just after our own American Revolution, during Thomas Jefferson's first term as president—occurred in the Caribbean nation of Saint-Domingue. Its French colonists had established a thriving, plantation-based economy through a combination of enslaving local people and massive slave importation to produce sugar, coffee, indigo, and tobacco for international trade.

At its peak, historians agree, Saint-Domingue was the most profitable colony in the world. But for thirteen years, beginning in 1791, the land's natives rose up and carried out the only slave rebellion to create a sovereign nation.[4] Among the victorious indigenous population's first acts was ensuring that their land would never again be known as Saint-Domingue, the name their French oppressors had given it.

It would again become, and forever remain, Haiti.

Haitian independence became official in 1804 but the need for revolution goes on, as Haitians struggle for a freedom only economic

---

4   "Laurent Dubois, *Haiti: The Aftershocks of History*, Picador: reprint, January 8, 2013.

independence can bring: freedom from poverty. And no one is fighting harder to help his fellow Haitians secure that freedom than Samuel Darguin.

Sam, Ginette and David...all three parts of the S4S model together.

The thirty-five-year-old founder and director of the Haitian-American Caucus in Haiti, Sam left New York City for good when he moved to Port-au-Prince to help rebuild the country of his parents' birth after the devastating earthquake of January 2010. The temblor killed at least one hundred thousand people; Haitian government estimates range from twice to three times that many.

Sam's father founded the Haitian-American Caucus (HAC) as part of his work in the United States and in Haiti. But as Sam's commitment to Haiti deepened, he established HAC-Haiti as a separate organization.

HAC-Haiti made its community center and school available to house earthquake aid workers and as an operations center for relief organizations. After the immediate impacts of the earthquake had been stabilized and many of the relief organizations had moved to more permanent homes in the capital of Port-au-Prince, HAC, with Sam's hands-on leadership, brought renewed energy to its founding mission: the development of the Haitian community through sustainable solutions to the extreme, cyclical poverty which has plagued the nation since it won independence.

"It started with a conversation that eventually involved farmers, single parents, adolescents, and unemployed men, matriarchs, and school children," Sam told me.

"After weeks of talking with the community about the issues affecting their families and learning about their goals and passions, we concluded that people needed quality, affordable primary education, professional development opportunities, economic empowerment opportunities, and improved public health," he explained.

"Since then, HAC has worked to provide such opportunities to the community of Croix-des-Bouquets, where we are based, and to rural communities around the country."

HAC now operates a kindergarten, primary, and middle school (with a high school in the works); adult literacy, computer, and English language programs; and professional development courses and workshops. It also runs clinics and facilitates public health trainings.

Then there are HAC's economic empowerment activities, in which shoes, the very same ones you donate to S4S, and which we ship to Haiti, play a pivotal role.

ONE HAND—FOOT?—
WASHES THE OTHER

Before its affiliation with Soles4Souls, HAC-Haiti's economic development efforts focused mainly on extending micro-loans to aspiring entrepreneurs. The loans, at reasonable interest rates, filled a crucial need in Haiti—where opportunists with less-than-noble aims loan money to the impoverished at exorbitant interest rates. This makes achieving profitability difficult, if the ventures can be sustained at all.

Yet even when HAC began offering very-low-interest micro-loans, it did nothing to change the hit-or-miss nature of micro-entrepreneurship itself. That's because many of the businesses begun by loan recipients—like agriculture, food, and beauty products/services—had low margins.

Compounding this was the fledgling entrepreneurs' lack of business skills or training, which increased the odds that their business would fail, with the loan not repaid. Sam didn't know it when we met in early 2013, but he needed a solution that tipped the odds of a new business's success in the borrower's—and thereby, HAC's—favor.

The answer, of course, was shoes. And while it seems like a great decision now, it was far from a foregone conclusion. It took a full court press from me and the S4S management team to get him to try his first shipment. Because not only did we believe it would be good for Sam and HAC, this was our first step in what we now call "direct micro." We believed that if we could cut out all the middlemen who were keeping the small entrepreneurs from being successful, we could dramatically increase these women's financial outcomes. We needed this as much as they did.

Sam was reluctant to get involved because his expertise was in vetting borrowers, not being a supplier. It took some persuasion, and some research in the local markets, for him to recognize that this was a real opportunity—for his clients *and* for HAC—to generate a new revenue stream.

"It took me some time to adjust and to really understand the market in Haiti, and how to really have the most impact on the most clients," Sam said. "After some trial and error, some mistakes, I think I finally got it down pat, where I'm able to really fine tune our model of providing loans, but also of providing loans and shoes, to where the women that we are servicing can really go out and see a benefit from that to help their families.

"For the first couple of months," Sam continued, "we were certainly underestimating the potential of the shoe market. So, I think that's one thing that looking back I said, 'Wow.' We took some time to really get that solid, to really understand, in a country that doesn't produce any shoes, the actual value of a pair of shoes—and what that does for the person that is selling it, for the person who's buying it, and the impact that it could have on the entire country."

It also boosted HAC's ability to serve its clients' other needs. The organization now has funds to build another floor on its school, which allows it to accept two hundred and fifty kids a full year ahead of schedule. A year of education and a guarantee of at least one hot meal five days a week is a very big deal; for many children in Croix-des-Bouquets, the meal they receive at Ecole Shalom is the only one they get each day.

"Besides the potential of the shoe itself," Sam said, "I think it's really using this ability that I now have; not just simply being a micro-loan distributor, but having shoes to offer. I would really like to use that as a way to get more folks into our programs, for things like health care, for things like literacy. To really use the shoes as a way to empower and to assist more women. Knowing that the women will come to buy the shoes and we can also make sure they know how to read and write, how to take care of their businesses, how to manage their family and their family's finance."

Sam is talking about the foundation on which the sustainability of any human endeavor rests: knowledge, gained through education, training, and experience.

ANOTHER VOICE

GINETTE DERISIER
MICRO-ENTREPRENEUR

"Before, I was selling rice, beans, oil in the marketplace. But with those things, you really don't see much of a profit. And then I had a friend that suggested, 'Hey, why don't you try shoes and see if you could do better for yourself?'"

We were standing outside the modest home Ginette had begun building, thanks to her hard work selling shoes.

"Now, I'm able to support myself, support my family. I'm able to send my third son to school, and to help my husband out when things are tough on his end. There are always more people who want to buy more shoes than we have, so more shoes would always benefit me and help me get ahead," Ginette said.

"First and foremost, the shoes that we get at HAC [provided by S4S] are top quality, and it's not too far from where we live. If not for that, then we have to go very far away to purchase shoes and the quality is just as not as good. When I first got started, I was only able to buy one box [of about one hundred pairs]. Now, I'm able to buy three, four, sometimes five boxes. The reason I like purchasing shoes from HAC is because whenever I purchase shoes there, I am sure to make a profit."

She gestured toward the house rising nearby. "I have this construction on a new house that I've started, that's taking me some time. If I had a more consistent supply of shoes, I'd be able to finish the construction of my house much, much sooner. Also, my son just entered university this year and is supposed to be there for five years. So with a constant supply of shoes, in five years, my son would be graduating from university." The pride on her face spoke volumes.

Ginette standing in front of her still-under-construction home.

"I'm going to pray that the people in the United States understand the real impact of shoes. They help my family a lot. If they continue to send shoes, I guarantee you, in about a year, year and a half, my house will be finished."

Then Ginette turned to me. "I'm so embarrassed to think I'm standing out here in this hot sun. The next time you guys come, I'll be able to receive you in my house and not outside here in the sun. If there were no issue of the quantity of good shoes available, I would tell a lot of other women like myself about this program and a lot of the women that you saw in the marketplace; they've purchased at HAC at one point or another. It's really a matter of quantity. So if there was the quantity, certainly we would be able to get a lot more women into the program and buying shoes."

FAR-REACHING EFFECTS

But how many lives can shoes really impact? I asked Sam that very question.

"I would be comfortable in saying for every woman that we assist with shoes and with literacy and with business management, there are at least twenty people that benefit," he replied. "And I know for HAC, the amount of women that we have that are specifically doing shoes is about four hundred, so if you add those up, four hundred or so women impacting at least twenty people, between family, friends, and neighbors, it's a pretty big number."

Eight thousand, to be exact.

"I'm very, very proud about that, because it's not just based on what I hear. When you spend some time and you talk to these women and you go to their homes and you see their kids and you see their families, you're like, 'Wow, these people are really progressing,'" Sam said. "They were not in this place when I first met them. And to really be able to see that concretely, where it's not just hearsay but you're able to go and experience that and you live that, is an amazing thing."

Sam wasn't finished, not by a long shot. "The power of one pair of shoes is incredible, life changing, empowering—those are just some of the words that first come to mind. One pair of shoes that gets down here to Haiti and that a person is able to sell helps their entire family."

I asked Sam what he'd say to prospective S4S shoe donors and supporters in the United States.

He said, "If you could, imagine that one pair of shoes that you donate in your closet is helping put food on somebody's table tonight. It's helping send a kid to school this morning. It's helping someone who is laying brick on their new house. Just from that one pair shoes. It may seem small, like, 'Well, okay, I don't need these shoes anymore. Let me donate them,' but the amount of people that are being empowered in a positive way by that one pair of shoes is incredible."

I wondered how big Sam thought the HAC program could become with shoes as its key component. He answered with a term familiar to those who have spent some time in New York.

"When I look at what we're doing now and how many folks [it affects], it's empowering, I'm thinking, the potential is humongous," he said with a grin. "We already have an outlet now in Cap-Haïtien [to the north], and there are ports in the south of the country. Miragoâne, Léogâne, these are potential ports where shoes can come in, and where HAC can set up an office to train women, and to create the micro-loan process."

Sam's excitement was palpable. "If we're empowering four hundred women now, imagine if we're able to empower eight hundred, or a thousand, or two thousand. Of course, it's easier said than done. We need to have more shoes, we need to have the personnel to really manage that, but I think that's something that we are excited about. Because I think, again, seeing what that pair of shoes does, and the ripple effect that it has from mother, to child, to husband, to aunts, to sister, to neighbor is just incredible.

"It's really empowering folks to *do* for themselves. To really take control of their own destiny. And I think when they have shoes, and they're able to go to the marketplace and they're bringing home the bread, they're bringing home the bacon, as we like to say, and I think that's very, very empowering."

When I asked why HAC's entrepreneurship programs are focused on women in particular, Sam responded, "In Haiti, and I'm sure this is true in a lot of other countries, the burden really falls on the women," Sam told me. "Besides the fact that in a lot of households there isn't a father to begin with, the ultimate responsibility for feeding and taking care of the kids falls on the women, even in those with a dad or other male figure."

"So, with that in mind, when the women are in the marketplace, earning for themselves—that's more of a reason for them to keep on fighting, to keep on pushing, because they know at the end of the day, they're ultimately responsible to make sure that the kids are fed that evening.

"Don't get me wrong," Sam continued. "There are great men here and there are great fathers here, but even with a working father that's maybe doing construction of some sort, the income is just not enough. So if dad is unable to bring in enough, someone has to add income, and usually it's the mothers who do that. Plus, we've just had great success with women in general.

"I think they're the ones who really want to advance. It means something to them when they go to their child's school and, for the first time in their entire lives, they're able to sign their kid's report card," he said, referring to the impact of HAC's literacy programs.

"Signing your kid's report card for the first time—for a lot of us that seems like, you know, nothing. But for someone that doesn't know how to read or write, who wouldn't even recognize their name if they saw it written somewhere, that's powerful, right? To be able to manage a business and write down numbers and create a budget, that's a big deal.

"That's why we choose women. They're more reliable. The burden of the family, especially in Haiti, ultimately falls on them. They're the ones that, in spite of everything, in spite of political instability, natural disasters, the buck stops with them. And they know that, and they take that with strength, with power. They take it head-on."

Then Sam introduced me to living proof.

ANOTHER VOICE

MARIE-ANGE ESPERA
MICROENTREPRENEUR

I have been selling shoes since 2013. My business is why I could build this house.

My biggest fear, whenever I go to get shoes at HAC, is that there won't be enough merchandise and I'll have to go and purchase shoes elsewhere. The risk is much higher that way, the potential to lose my money is much greater. But since I've been with the HAC program, I've been able to accelerate a lot, so my biggest fear is not being able to have the quality of shoes that I've been getting to continue progressing for me and my family.

The HAC program has brought two very positive things. One, I'm no [longer] getting money from loan sharks. I started with a loan from HAC, my business grew, and now I don't even need a loan, which means I keep more of what I earn. It's exciting; I went from taking money with an interest rate that's way too high and having to buy shoes that are subpar, to [having] a fair loan to no loan and getting good quality shoes. It's a win-win.

Marie-Ange negotiates in the market.

When I take the shoes from HAC and sell them, I am able to save the profit. That lets me buy the land, and I'm very proud of that because almost no woman owns land in Haiti. And now we live in the house that shoes built.

We are eight people now living in the house; we have three beds. It's technically not finished yet, but I'm very happy because I have my own house. I'm very proud of myself. I don't have to go anymore to the loan sharks to borrow money. I don't have debt.

The HAC program is why I could buy my own land and build my own house, and has allowed for much more. For example, before, if someone maybe is sick in the family, maybe we couldn't go to the hospital. Now we can.

When you support women in Haiti, you support an entire family, and even more people. I'm able to help my friends, maybe not at 100 percent, but at least at 40 percent or so, if they have an emergency. It's a ripple effect. Now I can help my daughter, my grandkids. It's not just the immediate family, but the extended family and neighbors that I can help support.

I am from Jacmel, in the southern part of the country. Because of my shoe business, I have enough money in the bank that when there's a family emergency, I can send money to support my family there. So to me, supporting women is the absolute right way to go. You see me, one individual woman, but there are dozens of other people benefitting from my success.

A lot of my clients are very supportive of me because when they get the shoes from me, they're also able to support their own families and send their own kids to school. That's another thing that makes good product important; my merchandise doesn't stick around. Once I get into the marketplace with my shoes, they're the first to go, because my quality is the best.

Besides the shoes, HAC's micro-loan program helps us. My husband is in construction. Sometimes he goes weeks, sometimes a month, without any projects. When that happens, I can get a micro-loan to keep the family on the right track if necessary, and when he's working, we are able to even save some money for a cloudy day.

As long as there's a reliable supply of shoes, in five years, my entire house, including the roof, will be in concrete and not in tin. All of my kids will be done with their high school and have at least two years in university.

It can be the same for other women who are able to come through the program and start getting and selling shoes. Their life will never be the same. They will advance; their lives will take off! Other products I'm selling stay in my hands for days, for weeks. I can never see an actual turnaround. With the shoes, it's "hot off the press." Once I get them the marketplace, they sell.

I am awed by the resiliency of the Haitian people. Less than a decade after a catastrophe of unimaginable proportion and several devastating hurricanes, they remain as determined as ever to fulfill the promise of the revolution that secured their freedom.

In pursuing lives free of poverty, Haitians are writing the next chapter of their nation's proud history—a fact not lost on Sam.

On the HAC website, he puts it this way:

> *We have seen first hand the differences between relief and development. Relief, although needed in times of emergency, works against sustainable change to communities by creating dependencies on aid. Development, focused on education and access to resources, and spun from the community itself, helps empower individuals to create the change that will build a stronger Haiti.*

I couldn't help but notice that word again: *empower.*

"What I'm proud of the most," Sam says, "is that I'm able to see so many women, in particular, raise themselves out of poverty. A lot of them were in a very miserable situation, and now [are] able to send their kids to school, support their families, and receive health care, all because of a carton of shoes that we were able to provide them. If we were able to really build this momentum, I think it would be life-changing for Haiti. Haitians need to be empowered. Haitians need to be given the tools to do for themselves, to buy their own food, to build their own homes, to send their kids to the school of their choice.

"That's the pride of the Haitian people. That's the continuation of the 1804 revolution that people here still talk about. It's not over." The fierce commitment to independence is evident at every turn in Haiti. These folks just don't give up, even in the face of relentless natural disasters and human-caused tragedy. It means something more than I can describe for a Haitian to be Haitian.

But as clear as it is there, in other parts of the world, it's murkier and more complex than I could have imagined. So let's head to one of those spots to explore a place that, in some ways, doesn't really exist: Transnistria.

CHAPTER 5

"AN INVISIBLE LAND"— TRANSNISTRIA

The challenges facing Haiti and Honduras are profound, but at least you know where you are when you're there. Halfway around the world lies a land where nothing is as it seems. It's called Transnistria.

If you've never heard of it, you're not alone. Few Westerners have. That could be because this tiny, elongated region comprises just 1,600 square miles. It's smaller than Delaware, and just a bit larger than Rhode Island.

More likely, you've never heard of Transnistria because it has not been recognized as a sovereign land by the United Nations or by any UN member state, though it declared independence in 1990.

Soles4Souls partner Mark Fashevsky arrived in the region as a child, when his parents moved to Moldova from Ukraine.

Both countries were Soviet republics at the time, but Moldovan culture was strongly influenced by Romania to its west; so strongly, in fact, the vast majority of Moldovan "Soviets" spoke Romanian. With the dissolution of the USSR, Mark told me, the country quickly embraced its true identity.

"Moldova changed their alphabet from Cyrillic to Latin. But Russians in Moldova decided to go their own way, and civil unrest escalated into civil war," he said.

The violence ended in 1992. More than a thousand people lost their lives, and Ukraine's 1991 declaration of independence left Soviet loyalists in Moldova without a nearby alternative. So they created their own land: Transnistria.

It lies on a narrow frontier, with Ukraine to the east and the Dnister, the river from which it takes its name, to the west. Transnistria is thirty-two miles from end to end, and eight miles across at its widest points, and all these years later the cease-fire itself remains the only thing to which all parties to the fledgling country's struggle for independence have agreed. The Soviet loyalists who founded it—and critically to Mark's work, their progeny, more than a half million people in all—have lived in the enigma that is Transnistria ever since.

"It is like an invisible land," Mark said. "You have Transnistrian identity, Transnistrian money, stamps, and everything, which is not recognized outside of Transnistria."

That means people born in Transnistria, as far as the rest of the world is concerned, don't "officially" exist.

"You need a set of documents if you want to travel," Mark said. "Everybody needs a Russian, Ukrainian, or Moldovan passport, and if you don't have it, then you're basically locked here."

The ramifications are both predictable and unfortunate.

Transnistria's government runs a dozen orphanages, each housing between two and three hundred children.

"We have a vicious circle," Mark said. He explained that after "graduating" from the orphanages—which provide the children with room, board, and schooling, often from birth—sixteen-year-olds with no practical life experience are suddenly expected to fend for themselves in a small land they cannot leave.

"By the time a child leaves the orphanage, he or she is very unequipped, very poor, no work ethic, nothing," Mark said. Many girls end up in prostitution. Boys get involved in petty crimes and end up in prison. "It's just a common story."

Transnistrian orphan girls—those able to avoid human trafficking—too often wind up with orphan boys. Before long, they become a family—but, typically, not for long.

"With no job training, the boy either abandons them or ends up in jail," Mark said, "and the girl, also unskilled, has no means for supporting the children."

Many of the children wind up in orphanages, just as their parents did. And the vicious cycle begins anew.

"FIVE POCKETS," MANY IMPACTS

Today, Mark runs Help the Children (HTC), a not-for-profit Soles4Souls partner dedicated to helping Transnistria's disproportionate population of orphaned youth.

HTC operates a chain of thrift stores throughout Transnistria. The profits allow it to pursue a dual mission: getting orphaned kids into foster families, and providing Transnistrians, particularly young women, with job opportunities to help them lead successful lives.

The effects of such work in a place like Transnistria, where unemployment and poverty run rampant, are immediate and profound.

Called "Five Pockets," the thrift stores go beyond helping to fund HTC's work. They provide good-quality shoes, clothing, and other essentials to all Transnistrians at affordable prices. Still, it's the stores' key role in disrupting the vicious circle Mark described that motivates him and his coworkers at HTC.

"We always bear in mind the social responsibility that we have," he said.

HTC's dedicated work in fulfilling that responsibility has brought jobs and foster care to a country that desperately needs both. Later, we'll meet Ana Dovgaliuc, who benefited from HTC's dedication to helping at-risk women, and became a key member of the organization's foster care team. But first, let's learn how Five Pockets itself came to be.

Mark was introduced to the thrift store model on a visit to Northern Ireland. He had worked in the humanitarian field for years, receiving containers of donated goods and distributing supplies to the needy.

"We still do this part of the job," he said. "We still partner with some of the agencies in the US and Europe when we do humanitarian assistance. But when I was in Northern Ireland, somebody told me about this thrift store concept and I thought to myself, this is something we can do here. It would create job opportunities, which is very essential for us, and it would also help us to run some programs for the children. So in 2009, we opened a small kiosk. We had some of the leftovers from humanitarian aid that had come in, and we got permission to sell them."

People started to come—and to buy. The kiosk quickly grew into the first Five Pockets shop, and the model was a success right from the start.

"We opened another one, and another one," Mark said.

It proved a perfect fit for Transnistria, and proved yet again that shoes change lives. In a land where every internationally non-negotiable ruble counts, Transnistrians can purchase durable shoes and clothing, supplied by S4S, at prices ranging from five to ten US dollars.

"People liked it because it was a good-quality product," Mark said. "It was sold very inexpensively, at an affordable price, and we just mushroomed."

Mushroomed is the right word: less than a decade after its start in a lone kiosk, Five Pockets now boasts twenty-five shops throughout Transnistria.

"Soles4Souls is our strategic partner," Mark said. "We receive shoes and clothing, and even if people are poor, they still like the brand names that come through occasionally: Forever 21 and Vans. People like it a lot. They can buy them inexpensively, and it helps us in our PR. S4S has supplied quite a few products that were not available here before we started the thrift stores."

Back then, Mark says, street markets were Transnistrians' only option.

"They would just go and pay probably three times or more than they pay here, for very poor quality products," he said.

Purchases made in Five Pockets stores help customers navigate the unique economy that Transnistria's quest for independence created. But the Five Pockets stores also help fund HTC's foster care program, the benefits of which extend much further.

"The Transnistria model of government-run orphanages is not really a good one," Mark said. "A child needs to live in a family."

He knew what had to be done, but in a land challenged in so many ways, introducing foster care was difficult. HTC started and administered foster care programs prior to opening that first kiosk, but once Five Pockets took hold, those services took off.

"We were pioneers. We were trying to encourage people to become foster parents. But we also realized that not all children would end up in a foster family. Some would have to go through the orphanage, then become self-sufficient."

Today, Five Pockets stores "produce the funds that we set aside to run the foster operations," Mark tells us, "helping the families, looking after the orphaned children, and helping the teenage girls to go through foster care. The girls would be the most vulnerable. The prostitution, I mean, everybody talks about prostitution in Eastern Europe, and it is a common thing here: money at the expense of your health. People prostitute themselves willingly into places like Turkey or elsewhere just so they can get out of Transnistria. And they just end up in the streets."

Among those who stay, orphans have it especially hard. "For an orphan girl to find a job in a dog-eat-dog world is almost impossible. The unemployment rate in cities is about 50 percent, and in villages it's almost 80 percent."

The Five Pockets stores offer jobs to the very population which needs them most.

"For us to give this opportunity to them is almost a life-saving undertaking. We spend a lot of time on these kids. They basically have no idea what it means to work fully—you know, dedicatedly, and it takes months and months to get the right attitude in place."

NOT JUST JOBS—*GOOD* JOBS

What jobs *can* be found in Transnistria typically pay a maximum of $200 (US) per month, "but to find such a job is very hard," Mark said. Of that salary, half or more goes to rent, leaving about a hundred dollars per month to live on.

"That would buy you some of the essentials," Mark said, "and the essentials in this case would be just the staple foods: potatoes and bread. Meat would be very hard to come by."

To make matters worse, the notion of a social safety net in Transnistria is just that: a notion.

"Everybody is on his own. I mean, the state as such is in turmoil. There's not enough money in the budget. People have to fend for themselves."

Jobs at Five Pockets pay above the $200 national average, and at last count, the chain employed upward of one hundred and fifty people. "It's considered a good job. It is stable," Mark said. "These jobs give people security they can rely on. You can make like $250 to $300 a month, which is a decent salary for a Transnistrian."

The Five Pockets story is one of precious few bright spots in an otherwise bleak economy. Single moms get top priority when jobs come available in the HTC stores, but children who have recently graduated from the Transnistrian orphanages are hired as well. Lena Ahremtseva was one of them.

ANOTHER VOICE

LENA AHREMTSEVA

HTC BENEFICIARY—AND NOW, EMPLOYEE

I was raised in a Transnistrian orphanage from birth to the age of sixteen.

About two hundred children lived in the orphanage. Our days were all alike. We would wake up, go to classes held there, and then we had free time for a couple of hours, but we could not leave the grounds. Then we had dinner and went to bed.

Lena outside one of the Five Pockets offices.

It was the same thing every day, and because many of the children do not behave very well, the teachers would tell them, "When you graduate, you won't do well. You will not be successful." Because of this, most kids don't believe in themselves, which also makes it hard.

After I graduated, I didn't know what to expect. I was coming from a village into a big city, not knowing what the future held. But I was lucky enough to become part of a Help the Children program, where I got different kinds of help—financial and emotional—and we were taught life skills, and [I had] a dormitory room by the college, where I lived while I studied to become a bookkeeper.

The people with Help the Children are positive. They gave me a good direction in life and good advice—to stay strong in school and continue my education. Not to give up. I'm very thankful to the people I met. They made me a part of Help the Children and I made new friends. All those years, I had people to lean on and to trust, and that helped me a lot.

In Transnistria, a lot of kids like me cannot find jobs. A lot of children from the orphanage, because they're orphans and have the stigma of orphans, nobody hires them. But Five Pockets hired me. I have my associate's degree in bookkeeping, and I'm now in my first year on the way to getting a bachelor's degree in accounting.

The quality of the products we sell is so good. Everybody likes the goods that are coming from the United States. We don't have that much variety here, usually. And we give many of these clothes and shoes to the orphanages for the kids. That's also important.

Children really like when there's somebody from the outside that comes and provides help and cares for them.

Lena's story shows how Help the Children's thrift store model of micro-enterprise is extending opportunities to young women in Transnistria that simply were not available to them before. The degree she is working to complete will allow her to participate in the country's challenging labor market, positioning someone who might otherwise have faced a lifelong battle with poverty for financial—and personal—success.

The chance to meet and talk with Lena (through a translator, as I don't speak any Russian) was powerful for me. Though shy, I could feel a confidence in her abilities and future that Mark assured me would not have been there just a few years ago. The combination of useful work and a supportive environment allowed her to flourish. While we saw plenty of examples of kids who might not have that chance, there are far more children in orphanages than HTC can put in foster care or employ; witnessing HTC's staff at work allowed us to see that this was not a fluke.

One of the reasons it's not left to chance is Mark's right hand woman, Ana Dovgaliuc. She knows this world in a deeply personal way and her story is yet another lens through which we can understand the power of thinking for the long-term with local partners who see things the same way.

PIONEERING FOSTER CARE

Ana Dovgaliuc was born in Moldova prior to Transnistria's declaration of independence. That means she has a passport and the ability to travel to other countries with more opportunity. She briefly did so after high school but soon returned, and has played a key role in the development of HTC's foster care programs ever since.

"I've been working with Help the Children for the last ten years," Ana said. "We started with nothing. There was no help to the orphans in this country. The government was very suspicious about our work. They always wondered where our funds came from, you know, the funding and the finances, because we help the foster families. We sponsor children. We provide stipends to the kids. And the government gave us a hard time, asking us where the money comes from and who are our donors. 'Does it come from the United States?' They thought it was something political that the United States was trying to do in Transnistria."

It took time and persistence, but gradually, Ana said, the government's concerns were eased.

"We tried to prove to them that our goal is to help the kids and that we really care about the families who struggle, that are vulnerable. And for the last ten years we've got very good respect from the government. Mostly they help us and allow us to do freely what we do.

"In the past they would not allow us to come to the orphanages to see the kids. They were very strict about the whole thing, and so today it's better, it's much better. Hopefully, in the future we can become maybe an organization that is approved by the government to do what we do."

I asked Ana what such approval would mean for HTC.

"We would hope the government would fund our projects, because today they don't give us any funding. These state orphanages are very expensive. We calculated that if that money was used to place children into foster families, it would help many more children.

"It's very expensive to have a child in an orphanage. They have to pay the staff and keep all these big buildings and utilities, gas and all these things. But for some reason, they still like the system of orphanages and so they're not ready to move to the foster idea."

Fostering children is a fundamental shift in approach, but like Mark, Ana believes a family is essential to a child's success. Her own upbringing informs that conviction, and has guided her work with HTC.

"Our desire [is] to help the kids in these big institutions where they have nothing, to put them into Christian foster families or families who want to take kids and take care of them, because in the orphanages a lot of the kids end up when they graduate in crime, prostitution, without jobs and without knowing where they're going."

Though she was not orphaned, Ana might have faced a similar fate.

"I grew up in a poor family. My father [drank], he was an alcoholic. My mom hardly raised us because she had a very low income, and so when I finished school, I couldn't afford to go to university. And so I was looking for a job and I couldn't find any work here locally. So I had to go abroad for other work."

Ana said many adolescent girls in Transnistria babysit to make money, "but that's very much at risk, because human trafficking is so big in this country. You may end up in slavery somewhere in Turkey or other countries," Ana shared.

Her difficult childhood gave Ana insight into the challenges confronting Transnistrian girls who graduate from orphanage schools.

"At the age of sixteen they have nowhere to go, and no hope. They have nothing, no financial support. It's really hard to live in this country," she said. "Thank God Mark invited me to work for Help the Children. I was very young at that time, and so just with a vision, we started doing this work."

Ana's schooling provided her fluency in English. Combined with her compassion for the plight of orphaned Transnistrian girls, that created a powerful skill set.

"I began as a caseworker, visiting foster families. Today I do fund-raising and communications with donors and travel abroad [to] just share the need, telling people about Help the Children.

"We want more people to know about this country," Ana continued. "A lot of organizations don't want to come in to help. They think it's risky to come here. So our goal is to spread the word and go and speak about the need, to get more people involved to help us."

That work has paid dividends. HTC's vision for introducing foster care to Transnistria has become reality, complete with comprehensive training and support for foster families.

Mark and Ana take a rare break.

"Today, we have about ten people on staff. We go into different places, speak about the need, and we find families who want to take kids," Ana explained. "We teach them about trauma, about the children, how to raise them, what the differences are because they're orphans."

At this writing, about seventy children are fostered through the HTC program—one which helps foster parents surmount challenges wrought by Transnistria's "frozen" geopolitical status.

"People mainly don't take children into their homes because they're poor, very vulnerable," Ana explained. "Unemployment is so high that people can't raise their own children, so taking new kids into their homes is a challenge. So here we come, with financial support, so that these families can feel that they can take the responsibility to raise somebody's kids."

Foster children in the HTC program are typically sponsored at $35 per month. The organization works to find at least three sponsors to cover the $100 monthly stipend to a foster family for each child they take care of. HTC is responsible for getting commitments from three sponsors at $35 each to cover that cost. If there is a gap, HTC/Five Pockets covers the difference. Costs per child that the foster family commits to include funds spent for food, clothing, and housing.

"The [Five Pockets] shops cover a lot of administrative cost," Ana said, "so we are able to give the donations that people give for the children straight to the family, without holding any percentage for overhead costs. The shops help cover our administrative costs and also help the orphanages."

CHOOSING TO STAY

"A lot of the kids are orphans because their parents are alcoholics, or left the country looking for jobs abroad." Because she came from similar circumstances and left Transnistria herself for a time, Ana understands. "When these children graduate from the orphanages, we help them, mentor them, send them to school, help them to find a job—and here is another place where the shops help us a lot, because we can give jobs to these kids."

One one level, I find it surprising that Ana remained in Transnistria, since she possesses the one thing so many do not: a valid passport. But Ana operates on another level. She says she feels like her "calling [is] here." That if she were to "go to another country, who else will stay to do this kind of work?"

"There are really very few organizations that help children and families, and I just don't see the need [to move]" she said. "Maybe because I grew up in a family that was in need and I really had a hard time. I did not know what the future held for me. That makes me stay, but I was tempted many times to leave. I had a lot of offers for better jobs abroad and every time I was thinking, 'I will probably not be content even if I get more income.'"

Ana saw the next question in my eyes.

"Yes, I feel content," she said. "I really like what I do, and I see changed lives. There was one girl we put into foster care. When the psychologist asked her, 'What's your most memorable day in your life?' she said, 'When Ana came to the orphanage.' For me that was really shocking, but for her it was the most memorable day because she knew that I'm coming to find a home for her. That's what makes you work and give your time and effort; not the income.

"At the same time, when you give you get back. I'm not talking even about financially, you know, you help others and you get help as well. So a lot of people support me, help me, and I have enough income to be able to live here, so I want to help others as well."

Even when her workday ends, the help Ana extends to foster children goes on. "About four years ago," she told me, "we connected with some girls from the orphanage and they really wanted to go to my house and spend time with me, and so we ended up taking them with us. Today there's three girls that live with us."

Talk about giving back.

"It's just been a nice journey. Seeing how they were very uncon-fident, and very aggressive towards people, traumatized—and now they all graduated from school, from college, and they have an education. They all got jobs and they're very independent. They can move forward, live by themselves now. And we became their family," Ana said.

"The first Christmas and New Year they spent with us, it was very unusual for them because at the orphanage they don't usually have big events. And the orphanages are so isolated from the society. A lot of the kids don't get to go out much. They don't have the experience of going to the theater or ice skating or seeing things that a child in a traditional family would see. And so being with us they have experienced a lot of interesting things, and it was a joy for us to help them and mentor them."

For Ana, fostering Transnistrian children comes naturally. "I plan to continue, to take new girls at the age of sixteen, when they're very vulnerable. That reminds me of my life and my background, and I can see that I become an important person for them. So I like doing this and helping them."

Her work has brought the lives of Ana's mom and brother full circle, too. "My family accepts what I do and they got involved as well. I'm very glad, because my brother would also leave the country for a better job. But because HTC offered him to help with things like translating, transportation, and other things that are very helpful for the organization, he's happy to stay and also be involved."

Her mother, meanwhile, is showering Ana's foster children with the attention she couldn't offer Ana or her brother due to the family's difficult circumstances when they were youngsters. "She just loves these girls that come in, and she still can help them and teach them cooking and other things that they don't know how to do. I'm really happy they're both involved."

A part of Ana's story—the commitment to stay—is a thread woven through the stories of Raul, Sam, Ana, and, as you'll read in the next chapter, John Pasco. These are people with incredible skills, who speak multiple languages and demonstrate shocking tenacity … they could make it anywhere. Through a combination of pride, connection, and vision, they have chosen the hardest path. Yet it is the path that will lead to them having an impact not only on their own lives but thousands of others, for generations to come.

WORKING WITH REALITY

Like the circumstances which birthed the young "nation," daily life in Transnistria is fraught.

For youth stuck in this international limbo, making sense of it all is low on the list of priorities. Making it to tomorrow is challenge enough.

HTC's thrift store model of leveraging the inherent value of donated shoes and clothing to create multiple positive social impacts is a textbook example of working within on-the-ground reality to serve immediate needs, while addressing lasting ones.

Mark gave me a final, incredible example of what it takes to make HTC's model work: "We can't just go into a bank and take out a loan. Here, *everything* is done in cash. We don't have credit cards. People only take cash, and pay in cash."

HTC must take the Transnistrian rubles customers spend in its Five Pockets stores to the bank and buy US dollars, which can be "very hard to come by," Mark explained. "So we put the cash in our bank account and just wait for dollars to become available. It can be days. Sometimes weeks."

But in a country whose money is worthless outside its borders, there's no other option. Even with those constraints, Mark has built an organization that employs hundreds of people, bought an industrial property without a mortgage, and has developed the capacity to serve thousands. The only thing more stunning than how hard it is to do business in Transnistria is how Mark and Help The Children don't even think about leaving.

Mark doesn't complain about it or overthink it, any more than Ana wrings her hands over the realities young girls in Transnistria face. Mark and Ana work within Transnistria's singular reality for one simple reason: It's the only way to reach their objectives.

"To give this unique opportunity to people," Mark said, "to help them live and work in a safe, friendly environment, it speaks volumes to me. I really take delight in it. I don't do it just to make money, but to help people in my community. It's why I'm here."

Working with this team in Transnistria is a constant reminder of how "grit" is at the root of their successes. Staying when it makes sense to leave is almost never the rational choice but, as they've proven, the world is a better place for their decision to remain in such a complicated place.

What may be harder than staying, however, is going. We're about to hear from Jon Bart, an American scientist who passed up the chance for a comfortable retirement to go to one of the most challenging countries on the planet, Sierra Leone.

CHAPTER 6

GOING TO AFRICA IN A BIG WAY— SIERRA LEONE

"It seemed clear that Sierra Leone had the opportunity to become one of Africa's great success stories. I think it still has that opportunity."

— *Dr. Jon Bart, President, Village Hope, Inc.*

The number of people living in poverty globally has fallen dramatically in the last twenty-five years, with more than one billion people lifted out of extreme poverty since 1990. In developing regions, extreme poverty dropped from 50 percent to 14 percent by 2015, according to the United Nations' Millennium Development Goals project.[5]

A glaring exception, however, is sub-Saharan Africa. There, extreme poverty remains stuck at over 40 percent.[6] But there are bright spots, and the work of a US-born S4S partner in Sierra Leone is one of them.

---

5   United Nations, *Millennium Development Goals Report 2015*, (2015); *Human Development Reports: Sierra Leone*, United Nations Development Programme, 2014: http://hdr.undp.org/en/countries/profiles/SLE."
6   Ibid.

Depending on the criteria used in ranking them, Sierra Leone, at this writing, is among the bottom ten countries in the world in per capita GDP. From 1991–2002, the nation dealt with a devastating civil war and, just at things were getting better, an Ebola catastrophe struck in 2014. Its economy has been decimated. What commerce exists is highly extractive, primarily ore and diamonds. The fruits of these enterprises don't trickle down to most people—and that doesn't even begin to account for their environmental impacts.

In 2007, life events encouraged Jon Bart, a longtime research biologist with the US Department of the Interior, to bring his expertise to Africa's sub-Saharan west coast. No stranger to Sierra Leone, having worked there professionally and visited for many years, his move to changes things began with an agricultural project, Village Hope (VH), aimed at breaking the cycle of poverty. But he was looking to diversify VH's sources of income, for reasons we'll cover shortly.

Jon thought S4S could be a good fit, so over a six-month period he set up the infrastructure: a warehouse and a store in Freetown, Sierra Leone's most populous city. Simultaneously, Village Hope trained people on the ground to sell and distribute shoes to villages in its service area.

Within a few months, these efforts turned five shipping containers of new and gently used items—some shoes, some boots, some clothes—into one hundred and eighty jobs supporting at least one thousand people, plus a five-figure profit to help fund other VH initiatives.

Before retiring, Jon's specialty was applying classical survey sampling methods to natural populations. Under his leadership, Village Hope has done critical work in analyzing, documenting, and instituting the best operational practices for producing garri, one of the region's staple foods.

But before we hear more about him, I'd like to share the story of an amazing couple who made S4S's involvement with VH possible.

OTHER VOICES
PATTI *and* MILLEDGE HART
S4S MAJOR DONORS

MILLEDGE HART: We got involved in Soles4Souls because of Buddy. We have a very long-term relationship with him that goes back twenty-five years. When he told us he was thinking about joining Soles4Souls and we read what the mission was, we were delighted that someone of his capabilities could go to an organization like that. We knew he'd have a huge impact.

Once he was there and getting started, and Patti and I started the Hart Foundation, we thought there was no better opportunity than for our foundation and for Soles4Souls to collaborate on something. We looked at multiple different things with them, but with the mission of Soles4Souls, "Wearing Out Poverty," and the fact that Soles4Souls was not in Africa at all, seemed to us like, "If we're going to wear out poverty, we need to be in Africa and be there in a big way."

The proposal they gave us—helping Village Hope create a new revenue source to fund its programs—resonated with our philosophy and what we were hoping to achieve with the foundation, and it seemed like a perfect thing for Soles4Souls to go do. We were delighted to fund that.

PATTI HART: We were inspired by Soles4Souls' approach to sustainable change in a region. I think the leadership of Soles4Souls has moved the organization from primarily the distribution of second-hand shoes to creating sustainable economic change in different regions of the world. We were really inspired by that, and by the fact that, in many cases, they are empowering women in the process. We recognized the chance to create small but impactful, sustainable change, and that's one of the things that drew us to Soles4Souls. I think they're at a stage where we can have an impact, and they're going through a bit of a transformation themselves, and we believe in that transformation.

And I think Milledge's point about the opportunity in Sierra Leone is spot on. I mean, it's about saying there's so much poverty in the world, obviously even in our own country, as we know—but you can't impact poverty without having a foot in Africa in some fashion.

Our son serves on the foundation board with us, and we wanted our first gift to be meaningful, something that all three of us had a passion about, that we felt could move the needle. When you start foundations and you start spreading gifts around, you can lose a little bit of the inspiration that comes from giving if you don't really have an opportunity to feel the impact. We knew very early that feeling the impact was important for us.

We looked at a number of things and chose two gifts to give, and Soles4Souls was our first and our largest. Not because Buddy contacted us, though it didn't hurt that we've known Buddy for a long time. We've seen the impact that he's had on the world professionally, personally, from a not-for-profit perspective, and we like the story of what he planned to do with Soles4Souls. So I think it's a combination. It wasn't really a group outreach. It was years of just continuing to talk with him over a few glasses of wine about what he wanted to do with Soles4Souls, and we were really inspired by it.

MILLEDGE: Since Buddy went to Soles4Souls, we'd been tracking it. Patti's company did a shoe drive maybe three or four years ago. We've been involved in Soles4Souls and trying to help, but this was our attempt to do something meaningful, to have an impact on Soles4Souls and to have an impact in Africa through them.

PATTI: Despite the Ebola outbreak, which happened about a year before we started our foundation, we never doubted what we were doing with Soles4Souls. We actually probably went the other direction, saying okay, here's one more crisis that they had to deal with in the region, so providing a gift to give people hope and to give people a chance to create a small community economy that they can benefit from is even more important than it was before.

I don't think we anticipated the leverage that would come from Village Hope's other businesses being impacted at the time, the same time we were giving a gift. Not only were we able to start the program for [Jon Bart] to distribute Soles4Souls shoes, but it allowed him to remain afloat when his other programs were being impacted, and to keep people working. That was a timing thing that we could not have predicted in a million years. We'll take it, because I think it matters. Our response was never, "Oh my gosh, what have we done?" It was more, "Now, this region needs something like this more than ever."

I think it's just another reminder of how fortunate we are to live where we live and have the life that we have, and these are things we wake up in the morning and don't have to think about, thank goodness. And it's unfortunate that others do have to think about it. So, yeah, I think we were doubling down in our own minds, once we understood how stressed the environment was.

MILLEDGE: I think part of our philosophy, as well, is that there are so many things to worry about that you can get bogged down by that, with terrorism and disease and all these other things.

PATTI: Natural disasters.

MILLEDGE: Natural disasters, right, which we're experiencing all over the place. At the end of the day, Jon Bart's organization is a good organization, and Soles4Souls was able to help. And by giving resources to really good people, you're going to be right more often than not, regardless of the disasters.

Our philosophy is not to worry about everything. Our philosophy is to try to help those who can work through big issues.

PATTI: Plus, I think Soles4Souls is a great story. You look at a lot of work that a lot of not-for-profits do, and they're at certain stages in their work where you can really move the needle. With all due respect to some of the big global not-for-profits that are important, it's hard, as an individual, to make an impact. Soles4Souls is at that stage where one person's gift makes an enormous difference. So for people that find that to be an important part of their giving priorities, Soles4Souls is at that stage. We'd love to be an inspiration; we'd love to be the smallest giver to Soles4Souls someday.

It's no stretch to say Patti and Milledge Hart are two of my favorite people. Another is the beneficiary of their generous gift, Jon Bart—the CEO and president of Village Hope, Inc.

Jon became interested in poverty reduction as he was turning sixty. The career-long research scientist with the US Department of the Interior loved his work, but wanted to do something different in retirement. The parallels between his search and the Harts' criteria for their gift to S4S were clear.

"We're registered in the United States as a public charity, but here in Sierra Leone as an agribusiness," Jon said, elaborating on the programs he has instituted and oversees. "We work in rural communities, attempting to reduce poverty. Our strategy is to start businesses that provide good jobs, and to use any profits for community programs … no money leaves the country.

"I looked into a range of possibilities, but settled on poverty reduction fairly quickly—and on working in Africa, because that's where the problem has been the hardest," Jon said. "Then, while still working for Interior, I had an opportunity to come to Sierra Leone. This was in 2007. I investigated the country quite carefully, and even then, it seemed clear that Sierra Leone, which at the time was ranked as the poorest country in the world, had the opportunity to become one of Africa's great success stories. I think it still has that opportunity."

Like any good businessperson, Jon fine-tuned his project as it matured. "We came in with a very different approach than we now have, a rather typical donor approach. We built schools, dug wells, made toilets, ran micro-finance, a whole slew of things. But after a couple of years, it became clear that we could keep doing that for the next twenty years without really transforming lives. A different approach was needed."

Jon made a tough but bold decision. "We gradually shut all of those programs down. I spent a year studying, and then we began working on the business model, or what we call a charity business model: a charity that starts businesses to create jobs."

Instituting the new approach proved challenging—and bigger challenges were yet to come.

"We began the current approach in 2013. We moved to our current location in the northern part of the country, leased two hundred acres of land, and planted most of it with cassava, a staple crop for much of west Africa, to produce garri [essentially, cassava flour]. A year later, we were just getting ready to harvest when the Ebola epidemic hit the country. So we had to wait."

Jon said those working for Village Hope were never personally worried about Ebola. "There has not been a single non-health worker from outside the country who died of Ebola. It was not a risk to us and we always knew that, but the country was at a standstill. You couldn't move around. There were rules against congregating. You couldn't get fuel to run your tractor. We almost lost the farm during that time; only through hard work were we able to save it," he said. "So, in 2015, we were back and starting to build the processing facility for garri. We brought in tractors, we were ready to go. Our cassava was still good."

Cassava tubers, the source material for garri, can remain in the ground for up to two years and still be processed. Village Hope had time, albeit barely, to harvest the tubers and turn them into garri.

Then, another disaster struck.

"In late March, the entire farm burned. It destroyed all of the tubers," Jon said. "A firebrand was carried in on the wind from another farmer, who was burning his fields [a common land-management practice]. It was an extremely bad year for fire; a big bio-energy plant nearby lost millions of dollars' worth of crops. So, we were not the only one, and were very fortunate that there were no deaths among the people trying to fight the fire. But frankly, that was tough."

I find Jon's resiliency nothing short of incredible. Not only did he re-imagine and restart his enterprise, but somehow he didn't see the challenges as reasons to stop, as lesser men might have. Instead, they compelled Jon to press on; to fight harder.

Just as Milledge and Patti Hart saw the Ebola outbreak as further proof of the need in Sierra Leone, so Jon doubled down and continued to put one foot in front of the other. "At the time, we had a pretty good grant from Rotary International. So, we were able to program a lot of that funding and barely stay alive. But it certainly hurt us. There were times when we really thought we wouldn't survive."

That never-say-die spirit is one of the reasons we at S4S thought Jon would make a great partner.

"By halfway through 2016," Jon continued, "we were starting to establish other businesses than farming, and beginning to produce our garri from new cassava tubers, more than a year after the fire. Thanks in no small part to Soles4Souls, we're still here."

And the outlook?

"We think we're in a pretty good position," Jon said. "We feel we've got a bright future and that we'll be able to help a lot of people in this country." Indeed, the project already has. Village Hope created permanent or temporary jobs for more than one hundred and eighty people within six months of becoming an S4S partner!

I had to know what prompted Jon's huge leap, from what had been an agriculture-centered social enterprise to saying, "I have a good idea—shoes!" The short answer, it turns out, is "local knowledge."

"Our vice president for operations, John Pasco, who is himself a very successful local entrepreneur, told me that in Sierra Leone, you have to diversify because there are just too many problems," Jon said. "Too many opportunities for a flaming firebrand to come in and wipe out your whole farm. John helped us see that if you don't have other sources of income, you really are at risk."

ANOTHER VOICE

JOHN PASCO
VICE PRESIDENT FOR OPERATIONS, VILLAGE HOPE

Soles4Souls helps us greatly, because our people are in poverty.

We distribute the shoes from Freetown, where we have our store. We decided to send shoes to our people in the provinces because they don't have access to come in Freetown because of transport. So now we send shoes to cities and provinces, Port Loko and Kono and Kenema and Makeni. We have all those branches.

I am a contractor. I work for Village Hope to find construction jobs. We have different areas. We have cassava, we have construction, we have a welding shop, and now the shoes.

In Sierra Leone, contractors go to government offices and find projects, construction jobs. Recently they gave me a job, three months to build a primary school, but we worked for two months and everything was finished. The job was done through Village Hope, through our construction business. But Village Hope had to pay for all the expenses up front. So Village Hope loaned the construction company the money to finish this job and make money.

The Village Hope team.

Soles4Souls shoe sales provided the money for Village Hope to do the construction, and when the government paid me, I paid this money back to Village Hope. So Soles4Souls helps us greatly, because you cannot do something unless you have money. That's always the way it is in Sierra Leone.

Soles4Souls helped Village Hope so we can make all these businesses successful—the farm, the shoe stores, welding shop, and construction. And Village Hope helps my people.

"John's advice to have other sources of income was good," Jon Bart said. "We have made money from our welding shop, our construction shop and most of all from Soles4Souls. Honestly, if we had said no to that opportunity, there's a very good chance we wouldn't be here today, because Sierra Leone is a cash economy.

"If you run out of cash, your program doesn't die a slow death. It dies instantly. Thank heavens we had that support. Every day, our shoe store makes money—and every day, we spend it. So, I think diversifying to the level we did was the right course. I'd do it again in a minute."

I asked Jon what diversifying into shoes meant, given that all of his organization's infrastructure was in Masori, which is as rural a place as I'd ever seen; the fourteen-mile trip down a dirt road took almost two hours by truck.

"We feel very strongly about tracking and documenting our progress," he said. "To do that, you need a defined project area." Once again, Jon's research background shone through. "We have nine villages where we work. That's our project area. Our goal is achieving a large, long-term increase in the average standard of living within that project area. It's an ambitious goal.

"When we began to start other programs, we did everything we could to continue benefiting people within the project area. In the welding shop, for example, in Makeni—that is fourteen miles from the project area," Jon said, "but we bring all of the employees there from our project area. Almost all of the employees in Freetown are from Masori, too. We will hire from outside the project area, but only if we absolutely have to."

I wondered what problems Jon faced in growing the shoe business in particular. The size of the market? Capital growth? Human resources?

"There's all sorts of problems," he started, "but if I try to think of the real limiting factor, in all honesty, I'm not sure there is one. I can talk about the various problems, but I truly believe that every one of them is solvable."

Jon's understated resiliency and determination returned for a moment—and in the next breath, the cool, calculating analyst was back.

"Just to tick off the challenges, the market is depressed here, meaning the price people can and will pay. Sierra Leone is still among the poorest countries in the world. These people can't afford the kinds of prices people can in other countries. But our costs to bring things in are similar, although Soles4Souls has given us some breaks on price, and I thank you for that."

The "low-price, high-cost" structure is one issue. Training is another.

"We're working with people from the villages who have no background in running a modern business. It's going to take time to bring them to the point where they can take over. But we're finding that we can do it," Jon said. "Moses Kamara, the head of our accounting section, didn't know how to turn a computer on in January 2016. Now he is our financial controller."

I had the chance to see Moses in action. He took us through a number of spreadsheets detailing how VH tracks sales, profits, and inventory. He was entirely self-taught, through a book and an app he downloaded to his phone. All in less than a year!

Putting people to work in jobs that develop skills they can use for the rest of their lives: that's the clearest, most succinct explanation I can imagine for how S4S and its in-country partners are wearing out poverty. And Jon, quite literally, is doing it on a shoestring.

Then, as if he'd read my mind, Jon summed up the challenge of that work more beautifully than I could hope to.

"In the United States, the best and the brightest go on to become senators and CEOs. If they're born in a village in Sierra Leone, they basically stay in the village. But we can find those people and give them a chance. That's all they need," he said.

I thought of Honduras, Transnistria, Haiti—and realized that the same is true of the best and brightest all over the world.

"Are there problems?" Jon asked. "Yes. But I think we're going to be okay."

PART III

THE PEOPLE AND VALUES THAT ENABLE OUR WORK

CHAPTER 7

OUR SOUL: COLLECTORS

You've met some of our amazing direct micro-enterprise partners and have seen how the S4S model is wearing out poverty in countries around the world.

In this chapter and throughout part III, you'll meet a host of the people and organizations that allow us to pursue that objective; I also share the S4S values that underpin our work. But first, a little housekeeping.

It takes many people doing some very specific things at just the right time for a not-for-profit social enterprise like S4S to move literally millions of pairs of shoes and clothing items to places all over the world. That simply could not happen without three other key groups: our *collectors,* our *industry partners,* and our *indirect micro partners.*

At Soles4Souls, we count all of these people and organizations as partners, but if we didn't designate their roles more specifically with the above nomenclature, things around the S4S office (and this last part of the book!) would get awfully confusing, very quickly.

We're going to delve more deeply into some of Soles4Souls' amazing *collectors'* stories. These collectors are **volunteers** located throughout the United States, Canada, Australia, Singapore, the EU, and the UK, where they initiate shoe drives and, in many cases, serve as drop-off points in their locales. They gather the gently used shoes that provide the majority of inventory we supply to micro-entrepreneurs the world over.

Our *industry partners* are the manufacturers, shoe retailers, and other businesses that provide new product and/or support our efforts to secure and transport product. They are a powerful force in achieving our mission, and you'll learn more about them in this section.

S4S's *indirect micro partners* ensure that product arrives at its proper destination and document its distribution, but don't have the same job-creation focus as our direct micro partners. Which makes this is a great time to explain our two distinct micro-enterprise models: *direct* and *indirect*.

Direct micro-enterprise is the model at work in the countries we've just visited: Honduras, Haiti, Transnistria, and Sierra Leone. S4S also operates *indirect micro-enterprise* all over the world. It was our original model when brothers (and charter board members) Nelson and Paul Wilson launched S4S's micro-enterprise program, soon after the organization's founding.

Just as its *direct* cousin relies on *direct micro partners* like those you've already met, so *indirect micro-enterprise* is supported by *indirect micro partners*—logistics-savvy, for-profit distributors who ensure that we honor our corporate donors' requirements for which countries the shoes and clothes are allowed. Until we have *direct micro partners* in every country, we need them. Let me elaborate.

Say a company like adidas or Chinese Laundry agrees to donate product to S4S, with the proviso that it doesn't show up within their existing markets. That's a perfectly reasonable request. After all, if someone can walk into a market and purchase the same shoes that sell at full price just up the street at a fraction of the suggested retail price, that hurts the industry partner's profit margin.

Indirect micro partners support S4S's *indirect micro-enterprise* model by ensuring that doesn't happen. While their fee for this complex service takes some value off the top—making for a tighter profit margin when the shoes are sold—it doesn't diminish the opportunity provided to the entrepreneur who is transacting business.

Most companies who undertake this work have a different mission than S4S does; their focus is moving product. Nonetheless, we winnowed through a lot of them as we fine-tuned the basic micro-enterprise model and have found people who understand what Soles4Souls is doing.

These companies are for-profit and make no bones about it. But these are the same partners that stood by S4S when we were on the ropes, extending us cash way ahead of when we had product to send them. They helped to enable the success of our micro-enterprise model, so we've stuck with them, too.

Our move toward more direct micro-enterprise might mean less business for them in the short term. They believe, as we do, that if we can grow Soles4Souls overall in order to serve more people, they might have a smaller percentage of our business but still do more volume than they are currently. They'll be as important as ever as we work with more corporate product donors. Another win-win.

Before we go any further, I'd like to talk about how we measure impact. We've looked at many ways to track it but have been stymied by cost and complexity. Like good entrepreneurs, however, we kept looking for a solution and finally found it in the idea of measuring "economic impact." And, like most good solutions, part of its value lies in its simplicity.

We know how many shoes and clothes we're distributing and to whom. We know that there are different economics for each channel. We know that what we want to measure is how much of the economic activity stays in the country. So here's our model, and our impact, through 2020.

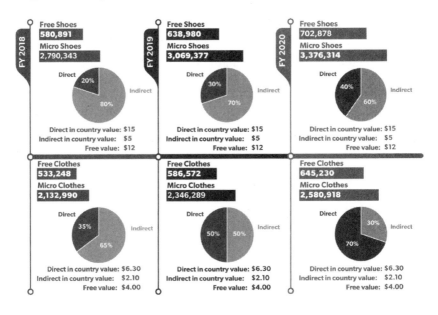

FY 2018

Free Shoes 580,891
Micro Shoes 2,790,343

Direct 20%
Indirect 80%

Direct in country value: $15
Indirect in country value: $5
Free value: $12

Free Clothes 533,248
Micro Clothes 2,132,990

Direct 35%
Indirect 65%

Direct in country value: $6.30
Indirect in country value: $2.10
Free value: $4.00

FY 2019

Free Shoes 638,980
Micro Shoes 3,069,377

Direct 30%
Indirect 70%

Direct in country value: $15
Indirect in country value: $5
Free value: $12

Free Clothes 586,572
Micro Clothes 2,346,289

Direct 50%
Indirect 50%

Direct in country value: $6.30
Indirect in country value: $2.10
Free value: $4.00

FY 2020

Free Shoes 702,878
Micro Shoes 3,376,314

Direct 40%
Indirect 60%

Direct in country value: $15
Indirect in country value: $5
Free value: $12

Free Clothes 645,230
Micro Clothes 2,580,918

Direct 30%
Indirect 70%

Direct in country value: $6.30
Indirect in country value: $2.10
Free value: $4.00

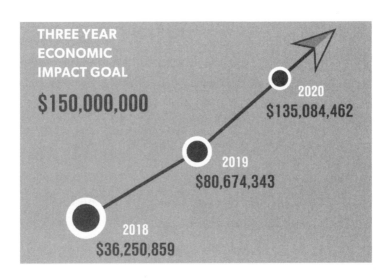

THREE YEAR ECONOMIC IMPACT GOAL

$150,000,000

2020
$135,084,462

2019
$80,674,343

2018
$36,250,859

In the near term, S4S has targeted a 60/40 split of *indirect* to *direct*—up from zero direct five years ago.

Based on that research, we've set a goal for the next three years of producing $150 million of economic impact by 2020, and a total of half a billion dollars from Soles4Souls' founding in 2006 through 2020.

Ambitious goals to be sure, and we are laser focused on this metric. It's also a little scary because we don't have every detail mapped out in terms of getting there. We are intentionally setting a target that will stretch us beyond anything we've yet achieved. That, we believe, will push us to serve more people, and to serve them better.

The more product we can push down the *direct micro-enterprise* channel, the faster our economic impact will increase, thanks to that model's emphasis on putting as much of the final sale price as possible in the hands of the entrepreneur. That's why I've shared the stories of our direct micro-enterprise partners and beneficiaries over the last four chapters.

However, the importance of *both* models, working in concert, is difficult to overstate. I've witnessed firsthand their combined effectiveness in wearing out poverty around the world.

Now it's time to meet some of the dedicated people and organizations who make both models possible—and learn why Soles4Souls work is so important to them.

OUR SOUL: COLLECTORS

"They don't have to do it. They don't have to host a shoe drive.
They don't have to bag 25,000 pairs of shoes like they do."

—*Kelly Modena, on S4S shoe collectors*

What motivates someone to begin asking their friends, neighbors, fellow churchgoers, relatives, and coworkers to give them their gently used shoes? And then, to *keep* asking?

These are questions I'm willing to bet you've never thought about. Before I joined Soles4Souls, I never had either. But now I know, and the answers are as individual as the people who do it.

In this chapter, we'll meet three of S4S's "super collectors." Three women—volunteers all—who started collecting shoes at different stages of life. Each has a unique story to tell; not just about why they got started, but why they've kept at it.

We'll start with someone I call a "super volunteer," for reasons you'll understand soon enough, but know she's collected more than five hundred thousand pairs of shoes!

It was January 2010. Haiti's catastrophic magnitude 7 earthquake had just struck when Michele James noticed an online ad: a local shoe store was offering customers a discount on a new pair of shoes if they donated a gently used pair to Soles4Souls.

ANOTHER VOICE

MICHELE JAMES
FORMER S4S COLLECTOR, COLORADO

I had never heard of Soles4Souls, and read a little bit about them. They were about to begin the "Travel with Us" program. I thought it would be an interesting thing to do, an opportunity to go to Haiti and distribute free shoes to those in need.

I had always wanted to do a trip like that, to go and offer help. Being who I am—I'm not a teacher, I'm not a nurse, I'm not a carpenter—there just didn't seem to be a way I would ever be able to, because I didn't have the skills the organizers of such trips are looking for. So when this opportunity presented itself, I called my friend and we signed up. We were in the first or second group to go to Haiti with Soles4Souls.

I've been there six times now. There'll never be another group like that first one. It was right after the earthquake, so we really didn't know what kind of accommodations we would have. We were prepared for the worst, but our accommodations were fabulous. Not by American standards, but by what we had witnessed around town. We had a bed, a mattress, a roof over our heads, and it was quite adequate.

The place not only had this dormitory, but there was a church connected to it, and a school. Every day we would see the children coming in, and we had the opportunity to give them shoes. It was just wonderful, seeing Haitian life unfold around us.

On my first three trips, we distributed shoes in a place called Cite Soleil, the poorest area of Port-au-Prince. We saw people in dire circumstances. Yet because of that, and in spite of that, I've never seen such gratitude, such resilience, and such kindness.

We began by washing their feet. Then they would be measured for their size, and we would give them a pair of shoes. And they would just be so appreciative and so grateful, and just give us a big hug and say, "God bless you." We did this for three days in a row. In that time, we distributed about fifteen hundred pairs of brand-new shoes, and it was very heartwarming.

I loved being with the people. On our last night, we were sitting around together, and our leader asked each of us about how our time had impacted us. And you think, "Well, what am I going to say?" I simply began weeping; I had no words for what I'd seen and experienced.

Michele James in Cite Soleil, Haiti

I came back to Denver and tried to think of something that might be of some help. I couldn't sleep. I couldn't eat. We had a family celebration in a nice restaurant, and I couldn't even order anything off the menu. I thought, "The price of this meal is the same as what somebody would earn in a year [in Haiti]." The equality wasn't there, and it was just breaking my heart.

I knew I had to do something, so I asked my sweet husband if it would be okay if I collected a few pairs of shoes in the garage. I sent one email about my recent experiences in Haiti to about twenty people, and asked if they had any shoes they were no longer using and could donate to this cause. Out of that I got a couple hundred pairs of shoes, but one of the people asked if she could share my story at her church. I was invited to come and speak, which I did.

Another person asked if it would be okay to put a box at Curves [a fitness franchise]. Well, gosh—I got twenty pairs of shoes in one week. If one Curves would do it, maybe another one would. And they said yes. I went to another, and another. Pretty soon I was collecting shoes from fourteen Curves locations each week.

I thought, "What about other places?" I noticed that a Whole Foods store in Denver was collecting shoes, so I went to others. Soon I had eight Whole Foods stores. Inch by inch, we increased our drop-off points. By the time I retired in mid-2017, we had eighty locations.

Today, we have maybe ten people who collect weekly from the drop-off points, but for the first five years, I did it myself. It got to the point where I couldn't spend all day, every day driving around picking up shoes and still have time to recruit other locations, do the book work, send out the thank-you notes, and all the rest. It turned into a big project.

My husband's business partner loaned us a warehouse. My friends came every day to help, but most eventually got tired of the project. I don't blame them. Sitting in a warehouse tying shoelaces together day after day can become a little boring.

I wrote a little spiel on volunteermatch.com, asking if anyone would be willing to help. As we grew, I kept using that resource to find more people to help out.

At the time, Las Vegas was the closest place where you could drop off a large load of shoes. My husband had a twenty-five-foot car trailer. We stored the shoes in the trailer until his business partner donated his warehouse. When we reached five thousand pairs of shoes, we planned to deliver them to Las Vegas and call it quits.

One school did a shoe drive and collected twenty-five hundred pair of shoes, which just blew my mind. Another person had been collecting shoes and acquired about two thousand pair, but lost her funding sources. She had no way to ship them, so I took them—and just that quick, the trailer was more than full. We had already outgrown our initial intentions.

One day I shared my thoughts with the staff at Soles4Souls. "Boy, it's very expensive to take all the shoes to Las Vegas. It's going to be costly." And they said, "If you collect twenty-five thousand pairs of shoes, we'll come get them."

At this point we were up to seven or eight thousand pairs. I'm Catholic, and it was almost Lent. The school had collected so many shoes that I started asking other schools about doing shoe drives during the Lenten season. We collected nearly fifteen thousand more pairs of shoes, and had almost enough for the first Soles4Souls' pick-up.

Changes evolved daily. After we were in the borrowed warehouse for several months, my husband's business partner was forced to sell the building. We were without a storage facility. I thought we were going to have to call it quits.

I wrote a short article for a local paper. Thirty minutes after it hit the mailboxes, this wonderful man, Carl Craig, called and offered me space in his building. It was a perfect match. The place was lovely, and his employees helped us load the trucks when they came.

That's one of the really cool things about this story: things just seemed to happen as we needed them to happen. We continued to grow, reached a few milestones along the way, and eventually hit half a million pairs of donated shoes. Some people would donate two pairs, some would donate a thousand. Every pair was important to the person that received it, and I think that's what kept us going—the importance of each pair of shoes.

In Haiti, the kids have to wear shoes to go to school, and every time a little pair of black shoes would come across our table, I would think, "Wow! Some kid's going to get to go to school just because of this pair of shoes." It made all the difference in remaining enthusiastic, day after day, because, as in any job, there were days that were kind of a grind. Understanding that a child's life is going to be changed because someone was kind enough to donate a pair of shoes is so important.

ON BECOMING A "RETIRED VOLUNTEER"

From 2010 until mid-2017, I lived about forty-five minutes from Denver. It's a jaunt, a twelve-hour-a-day job, every day. I'm seventy-one years old, and my husband is older than that. We needed to move to a one-story home due to some health issues, and I needed to take care of my husband. I just couldn't continue the day-to-day any longer.

The operation we'd built as volunteers was good enough that Soles4Souls said it would be worth investing some money in, to keep going. They hired Emory Dinner, and she's doing a magnificent job. Now it's a corporate facility; still the same building and everything, but the operation is a little bit different.

Some of our volunteers stayed, some have moved on. The people working with us very much care about the project. They remain resilient.

Soles4Souls has given me opportunities I could never have imagined. I've met so many wonderful people—not only in Haiti, but in the United States, too. Being seventy-one, how many opportunities would I have had to do something that impacts so many people? It's good for your soul, and makes your heart happy to do things that impact—in a good way—other people.

I'm not only speaking for myself. Several times, there were others who were older than me. Sarah's nearly eighty, Bob is eighty-one, and Wanda is seventy-six. I mean, we moved more than three hundred and fifty tons of shoes, and at times it was all a bunch of old folks!

From time to time, school groups came in to help, but for the most part, older people have time to do this. My career has passed, so it was wonderful to have a place to contribute. Countless people came to me to say, "Thanks for giving us an opportunity to give back. You read these stories in the news, and you would like to help, but you don't know how."

Shoes are a common thread that everybody needs, everybody understands, and goodness knows even I have more in my closet than what I need. It was a way to give back, and it was simple—very simple. And that was a very, very good thing.

MAKING COLLECTORS' WORK EASIER

As S4S's Director of Commumity Partnerships, Kelly Modena, couldn't agree more. Kelly worked closely with Michele James, and lives for helping people to see the difference that the simple act of donating shoes can make in the lives of others.

"This is something so easy," Kelly said. "Whether it's cleaning out your closet and donating your shoes or, if you're like Michele, rallying and influencing your community to do a shoe drive. So many people these days ask, 'What can I do to help?' We give them this super-easy solution that amounts, really, to just cleaning out their closet. They're going to do it anyway."

Kelly and her team work to coordinate thousands of large and small shoe drives globally. These generate all of the gently used shoe inventory S4S supplies to micro entrepreneurs around the world. A big part of her job is making the work of our volunteer collectors as easy as possible.

"Micro-enterprise might be a little hard to understand for those who are not educated about it, but *helping* is simple," she said. Then she just laid it out in her clear, direct way.

"If someone came to me and said, 'Can you give me $5, or the shoes on your feet?' I would probably give them the shoes. It's an easier ask! Honestly, it's a simple way to give."

In case you weren't already convinced, Kelly really digs her job. She is totally devoted to S4S volunteers.

"I just love Michele," she said. "I was her contact for many years before she retired. Just a sort of side story, to show how important it is for volunteers to know the impact they're having: when we started to really dig in to discover our impact, we found that one pair of athletic shoes sold in micro-enterprise can provide the seller's family with five or six meals, or x days of shelter, or y days of schooling—the numbers vary based on the country, but it's really cool to relay that information to somebody like Michele. She can share it with her volunteers while they're loading a truck, and it makes something that's so laborious much easier."

Kelly paused for a moment, then shared the bottom line. It's something all of us at S4S know, yet struggle sometimes to put into words. "They don't have to do it. They don't have to host a shoe drive. They don't have to bag twenty-five thousand pairs of shoes like they do. But they do, because they understand the impact."

We'll hear from Kelly again later. First, let's meet another S4S super-collector, at the opposite end of the age spectrum. Claire Baker is studying overseas and shared her story via email; her mom filled in some details by phone.

OTHER VOICES

CLAIRE FRANCES BAKER
and PAM BAKER
S4S COLLECTORS, MINNESOTA

CLAIRE: I was in seventh grade, 2010, and my religion teacher gave my class an assignment: we had to do a service project each month, starting in January and ending in May. For example, we could babysit and give the money we made to a local charity, or pick up garbage around our neighborhood.

These were all good things, but I wanted to do more. Dawn and Lee Shelton, family friends, were in the process of adopting two kids from Haiti. During their visits to the country, Dawn and

Lee would see kids wearing plastic pop bottles for shoes, crushed down and tied around their feet with a cloth.

The Sheltons asked why the kids had this type of shoe, and learned that their moms did not have enough money to buy more than one "real" pair. Shoes are required for kids attending school in Haiti; children without them stay home and make do with the pop-bottle "shoes," and the children "flip-flopped," taking turns going to school.

Dawn and Lee were shocked, and started an organization back at home called Flip Flop Fleet, to collect used shoes and send them to Haiti. When my service project came up, my mom mentioned Flip Flop Fleet and collecting shoes. I liked the idea because I had heard about the earthquake that hit Haiti and wanted to help, but did not know how. This was my chance.

I wrote down a plan of action covering the next couple months, and went to talk to my religion teacher. I planned to collect two hundred and fifty pairs of shoes from my school and church community, but my teacher said, "That is not going to be a big enough project."

I went home that day upset. When I told my mom what my teacher had said, Mom wrote an email and I got a yes about a day later. I do not know exactly what my mom wrote.

FROM PAM BAKER, CLAIRE'S MOM: I'll tell you what I wrote: "I would like to respectfully request you reconsider, because here's what it looks like." We detailed it more clearly for the teacher and got the parish priest and principal involved. The teacher humbly rescinded her decision.

CLAIRE CONTINUES: With the approval, I went to each of the eighteen classrooms in my school and talked to the students about donating their old shoes.

I was so nervous. I remember walking into the eighth-grade class and shaking, because here I am, this little seventh-grade girl, talking to these eighth-grade students about their old shoes. Well, it was a success, and by the end of the collection we had more than four thousand pairs. The power of being young is huge! But we also had a problem: more than four thousand pairs of shoes in my parents' garage.

MOM'S PERSPECTIVE: I am sitting with forty-five hundred pairs of shoes in my garage, in the middle of winter in Minnesota, and our cars can't fit in our garage. I can't put these shoes in a suitcase to be sent down to Haiti. I didn't know what I was going to do!

CLAIRE CONTINUES: My mom got a random email one day: "Do you have any shoes in the back of your closet you do not wear anymore?"

She quickly called the number on the bottom of the email, an organization called Soles4Souls based in Nashville. She talked to Pattie Graben, and since that one phone call back in 2010, our relationship has blossomed and grown in ways I never would have imagined.

MOM ADDS: Pattie said, "There's a drop location in Iowa," which was about three or four hours away. I decided to find somebody with a truck, and we went down and dropped off the shoes. That was our routine. We had collected those first forty-five hundred pairs, but once we started collecting, the shoes kept rolling in; we had no endpoint.

CLAIRE: After the shoe collection at my church and school, we were incredibly impressed with how easy collecting shoes can be.

I talked to leaders of local organizations—Rotary clubs, vacation bible schools, Lions clubs, and confirmation groups. The shoe collection grew and grew. I was so surprised by how the community reacted. Very soon I became known as "The Shoe Collector," and that's what I consider myself to be today.

I was contacted by a couple of television stations. They wanted to do stories on the project. We hosted community shoe drops around the Twin Cities, and they were broadcast live on the news. People would come to drop off their shoes. The project really took on a life of its own; there were always shoe collections going on. Our garage was almost always full of shoes.

MOM: Our garage *was* full and, thank goodness, our church came on board. They provided us with some space in an outdoor barn. About every four months, we enlisted the help of friends, got U-Hauls, and drove to Sheldon, Iowa, the drop-off location.

CLAIRE: Once I reached high school, I went to speak at other schools to ask them for their shoes. I started to get very comfortable speaking in front of large groups.

Recently I spoke to twenty thousand students at WeDay in St. Paul. It was an experience like no other. Before the event, I had to opportunity to go over my lines and get a feel for the size of the stadium and how my voice would project. On WeDay itself, the energy levels were buzzing high as my family and friends and I were escorted to the main floor to watch the program unfold.

It was surreal. I was a little anxious, but excited. When it was my turn to speak, I just took a few deep breaths and reminded myself that no one knows my story better than I do—and that these students wanted to hear about how being young is powerful, and that you can do anything when you set your mind to it.

THE PROUD MAMA: She stood on the stage with Buzz Aldrin. There were a couple of guys from Kenya who came up to do motivational speaking, and there was Claire to talk about shoes. It was an unbelievable opportunity for her to share the story and celebrate Soles4Souls.

CLAIRE'S "NOW": Today, there are annual shoe collections in the Twin Cities, and we receive the shoes. Soles4Souls provided us with a fifty-three-foot semi-trailer. We are now considered a warehouse location for Soles4Souls. We get phone calls from all over the upper Midwest.

I am a theology major on a pre-physician's assistant track. I attend a liberal arts college, which allows me to take a wide range of subjects and classes that I enjoy. And shoe collection definitely got me to think more about what is out there in this life. "How can I make a difference?"

Working with Soles4Souls these last seven-plus years has taught me to care for others, to ask questions, to smile, and to stick to what I know. This company has gone through so much, and my mom and I have been grateful to have watched it all come together. The people who work at Soles4Souls inspire me to continue following what I love to do.

I was fifteen years old when I first went to Haiti. That was years ago now, but there are pieces of that trip that I can remember like it was yesterday. The airport was like an old barn with a couple belts for moving luggage around. It was hot and smelly. Then we took two white vans up the mountainside to what would be our home for the next five days.

During the first distribution, we walked a little way down the hill to what seemed like a church community. They were singing and praising on the hot fall afternoon; their energy was captivating. There was a similar theme to all of the distributions that first trip. The children's smiles when the shoe slipped on their bare feet was contagious

Claire Frances fitting shoes in Haiti

Those smiling faces are what has kept my shoe "light" strong. I have traveled to Haiti with Soles4Souls four times now, and each experience has brought different stories and different perspectives.

MOM CONCLUDES: Soles4Souls—Buddy Teaster, David Graben, Tiffany Johnson-Turner, and [former S4S employee and still friend] Nicole Atnip—this core group of people nurtured the foundation that my husband and I have raised my daughter in, and they have provided her life's direction. They don't only impact third-world countries. They've impacted a middle-class young woman to become a person dedicated to a lifetime of international service.

At this writing, Claire Frances Baker's shoe collection efforts (with help from her family and many others) have netted more than 400,000 pairs of gently used shoes for S4S. Incredible.

SHOE (DRIVES) FOR ANY OCCASION

Kelly Modena, an S4S team member we met earlier in the chapter, leads efforts to make shoe collection as easy as possible for volunteers.

"We create shoe drive programs so we have something specific for different groups to offer. For example, we have the 25k Drive which allows people to 'fundraise' shoes instead of money, so they can travel with us. If they collect 25,000 pairs, they're awarded an international trip to distribute shoes to children in need."

Kelly's department designs drives for events-and groups-of all kinds. "We have a Girl Scout patch program, where the girls earn an S4S patch for collecting a certain number of shoes." Other programs include Barefoot4Them, which asks people to walk barefoot for a day, events for faith-based organizations, civic organizations like Rotary and Lions clubs, an Eagle Scout program, and employee engagement projects from Fortune 500 companies to those with just a few employees. In other words, there's something for everyone—from birthday celebrations to local activism.

"The Ten2Give program is a really cool one that helps people give back to their communities," Kelly explained. "If people collect ten thousand pairs of shoes, they win a custom shoe distribution to a qualifying organization of their choice.

"Ten2Give helps solicit shoe donations because people know that if the drive succeeds in getting ten thousand pairs, the homeless shelter right down the street will benefit—and the whole community is invited to come help." S4S procures new shoes for the distribution to beneficiaries of the selected organization, and sets up the distribution event.

"Another example," Kelly adds, is that "we'll research big companies that are super 'green,' that cite sustainability or recycling in their mission statements. Then we'll design and pitch them a Go Green campaign, in line with their business and philanthropic passions."

Kelly's department designs and motivates entire campaigns, then provides collectors with the tools and advice needed to make them successful. Her work shows how Soles4Souls' outreach efforts have matured since our early days, when we counted mostly on online advertising, unsolicited emails, and word of mouth.

Thankfully, it reached not only Michele James in Colorado and Claire Baker's mom in Minnesota, but another eventual super-collector: Pennsylvania's Karin Leaver.

ANOTHER VOICE

KARIN LEAVER

S4S COLLECTOR, PENNSYLVANIA

A friend showed me a brochure. I don't remember if her church was involved—but somehow, I heard about Soles4Souls.

We have six kids. We've always had extra shoes, so I just would send off a little box every once in a while with six, ten, twelve pairs. One year for Easter I thought, let me just extend this to my family. Cousins, aunts, and uncles, etc. I said, "Bring your shoes for Soles4Souls." And it was *hundreds* of pairs!

When the earthquake hit Haiti, I felt called to go, but thought, I'm not an engineer, a nurse, a doctor, or a social worker. I felt like I would be in the way.

I heard that Soles4Souls had started "Travel With Us" and was going to Haiti. I thought, *that's* something I can do! I've been washing feet for a lot of years, and I can certainly put shoes on people! I planned a party, Kick Off Your Shoes for Haiti, with a goal of collecting a thousand pairs. That seemed like a lot.

I invited people via Facebook and reached out to my email contacts, local people. Sadly, we canceled the party because our family suffered the loss of our pet that day, just before people were supposed to arrive. The party kind of turned into more of a wake.

My girlfriend stood in the driveway and said, "Chip and Karin and the kids don't really want to have people today, but feel free to leave your shoes." Well, that produced a mountain, nearly forty-three hundred pairs of shoes!

I was overwhelmed, in a good and a bad way. I mean, wow, what an outpouring of generosity, but also, I have to box and send all these shoes. I planned on UPSing them, but the cost was about a dollar a pair: $4,300. I headed for Haiti with no idea what I'd do.

MY FIRST TRIP, AND THE YEARS SINCE

I had no idea that my heart would be so pierced by Haiti. It was all so overwhelming.

I lived in Southeast Asia for a year after college; I saw poverty. I had also seen images of destruction. But [I had seen] nothing like the combination of poverty and destruction that was Haiti when we arrived.

We worked at a school called the School in the Mountain, literally built into the side of a mountain. We were seeing kindergarten through second grade the first day, and a balance of the classes the second.

That first day, a boy sat down in my chair, and I started washing his feet—and they were enormous. He was probably six feet tall and had these big, wide, mountain feet. I did not speak Creole at the time to ask how old he was, so John, one of the Soles4Souls guides and an American living in Haiti with a Haitian-American wife and their three sons, asked for me. The boy was fifteen and in the second grade. And I just thought, okay, I'm going to lose it right here. I'm going to start crying, and it's going to be terrible.

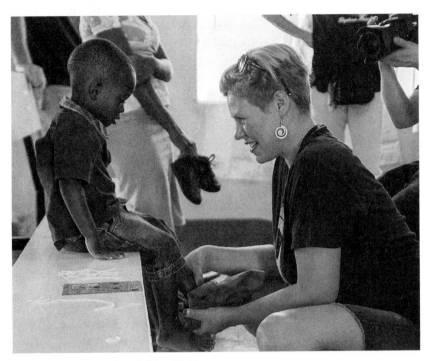

Karin connecting with a child in Haiti

And John said, "Don't be sad for him, Karin." He could tell I was getting upset. "Don't be sad for him. He is so proud to be going to school!" John explained that in Haiti, there's no shame for him. "They go to school when they can afford it, and he's so happy to be here in second grade."

When I got back from Haiti two weeks later, the local paper had done an article about my mountain of shoes, with a picture they must have plucked off Facebook.

I had two messages on my machine: One from the local Catholic church offering to include the shoes in a post-earthquake relief shipment. But I really wanted them to go through Soles4Souls. The other message was from a chick hatchery, Moyer's Chicks. My parents used to get chickens from them. I thought it was a very cool connection. They said, "We love to give back. We drive an empty truck down south every week and come back filled with eggs." I got them the address of the Soles4Souls warehouse in Alabama. It was just a few miles from where they were going! Amazing.

They sent a crew of people from their company. All I did was feed them dinner, and they palletized and shrink wrapped those four thousand-plus pairs of shoes.

They stored the shoes I collected and delivered them to Soles4Souls' warehouse for me—for *years*. I would take them nine or ten boxes and they would warehouse them until they had a truckload. Eventually, their shipping and warehouse situation changed and they couldn't continue, but it was so amazing.

Then I found Shepitex in New Jersey, a Soles4Souls indirect micro partner. I had a furniture store at the time, and used our van to take shoes to Shepitex. One day, Kurt, the owner, said, "You're here all the time. If I rented a storage unit in your town, could you collect more shoes?" I said, "Absolutely."

Now Kurt rents the unit and sends a trucker about every six weeks for a pick-up. We average about a thousand pairs a week. People find us on the Soles4Souls website. Everybody's got shoes. It's amazing.

When we load the truck, I post on Facebook, you know, "Looking for three volunteers to load the truck!" Then I'll post a picture and tag whoever [previously] volunteered. And, of course, their friends see.

It doesn't feel like work; it's just a time commitment. Every time I've thought, "I don't know, maybe this isn't going to be my area of serving," I'll get home and there's three bags of shoes. And I have no idea who they're from. I've become the Shoe Lady.

As Kelly Modena has said so well, the concept of micro-enterprise can be difficult to understand, but giving gently used shoes to support it is simple.

In this chapter, we've met three long-term volunteers whose commitment to Soles4Souls' mission of Wearing Out Poverty has allowed them to collect—literally—*tons* of shoes. They and all who work to further our mission have our sincerest, undying, and unconditional gratitude.

Next, we'll delve a bit more deeply into the workings of our micro-enterprise models with the help of some of the shoe industry's biggest supporters of Soles4Souls' mission.

CHAPTER 8

OUR HEART: INDUSTRY PARTNERS

Volunteers like those you've just met have collected millions of gently used pairs of shoes since Soles4Souls' founding. Their tireless work fueled the organization's initial humanitarian relief and micro-enterprise efforts, and continues to do so today.

But, as we have seen, S4S's poor job of explaining the evolution from its initial focus of disaster relief to its social enterprise work of today was due largely to a lack of transparency about its new business model. After local media reported that the organization was selling shoes, attempts to explain rang hollow to some longtime supporters. With all of the changes in 2012, we could fully embrace micro-enterprise—and get much better at detailing how it works.

We had to. Imagine walking into a shoe manufacturer or retailer and saying, "Why don't you donate your product, then let us resell it?" You're as likely to get thrown out on your ear as asked to explain the idea!

In this chapter, I'll introduce some of the shoe industry players who not only heard our micro-enterprise pitch but went all in. Their perspectives further illustrate why S4S chose this mission and shows how, by fostering micro-enterprise, these incredible companies and brands, along with many others, became crucial allies in our commitment to wearing out poverty all over the world.

THE BRAND WITH THE THREE STRIPES

Soon after adidas consolidated its North American operations in Portland, Oregon, Patty Goffe learned something that has since been parodied to a fare-thee-well in the eponymously named TV series, *Portlandia*: the city's residents are—shall we say—*quite* interested in how … well, *everything* impacts the greater good.

OTHER VOICES

PATTY GOFFE
COMMUNITY AFFAIRS MANAGER

and TAUNA DEAN
DIRECTOR OF SOCIAL PURPOSE,
ADIDAS NORTH AMERICA

PATTY GOFFE: When we migrated our employees to Portland, we had no formal community affairs or social responsibility role at adidas, outside of our headquarters in Germany.

My role was to liaison with the local community, to manage community affairs across the country, and to develop programs that reflect our brand's sustainability and community engagement activities so employees could contribute to our social engagement initiatives.

We finally had everybody in one place—Product Development, Product Testing, Marketing—all of which generate a tremendous amount of product samples. Often, these were being disposed of. Some of that was necessary; we couldn't give away prototypes, so they had to be shredded. But some samples could be donated; we just needed to formalize the process.

I started looking for a donation partner about the time Wayne [Elsey] was reacting to the South Asian tsunami, and to Hurricane Katrina. We wanted to redirect hundreds and thousands of pairs of samples to do good, versus heading for the shredder. Our other ambition was toward a sustainability component.

Knowing that Wayne came from the footwear industry and worked with a lot of other brands was appealing to adidas. His fast-track record of growing Soles4Souls made a lot of sense to us from both the people/donation side and the sustainability side.

That's where it all began. We were sending gently used product donated by our employees, sales samples, and product development samples that qualified for donation—which fewer did over time, as consumer product safety regulations tightened. With Soles4Souls, we began offshoring virtually everything. It really contributed to their micro-enterprise model.

Now it's been more than ten years, and Soles4Souls helps us identify how we further their mission and our own.

Beyond that, throughout the adidas Village here, we have high-visibility receptacles where employees can drop new and gently used products. We box and send them out regularly.

Tauna feels the love in Haiti.

TAUNA DEAN: I head the new team called Social Purpose. Our mission is to remove barriers to sports for underserved kids. Mark King, the president of adidas, was a big advocate that those of us who have benefited from sports pass it back to kids that may not have that opportunity.

One of the barriers is product and equipment. When employees have samples, they can connect the dots between our mission of getting kids that product—in this case, shoes— with what they have on hand.

So with those big bins around the campus, and the more we educate on the mission, the more people understand why we're asking for donations. Our employees are even more engaged and excited about fueling Soles4Souls' great work.

Last spring, Patty, my team, and I, and a few other employees went on a Soles4Souls trip to Haiti with [S4S Chief Operating Officer] David Graben. We'd donated two hundred thousand pairs of shoes prior to the trip, and were able to understand what Soles4Souls is doing in the space of micro-enterprise.

It was truly life-changing. We met a couple of the women in Haiti who had leveraged adidas samples to create a micro-enterprise, and to use those funds to support their children. One put three of her children through college because of her partnership with Soles4Souls. A lot of that was fueled by the adidas partnership. It was incredibly moving and impactful.

PATTY: Tauna said it, it was life-changing. I was super impressed to see the on-the-ground work that Soles4Souls has developed in Haiti, and now in other countries (e.g., Honduras, Transnistria, and Sierra Leone)

A lot of times when big brands make big donations—we've all seen in the media that the product doesn't always get to the right people in the right way. That trip really underscored for us that we're working with a credible partner that can really do the most good with our products.

They've also met our requirements about sensitivity to markets. There's been continuous communication; if they have questions about certain donations going to certain places, they've always contacted us to get direction.

Traveling with David to Haiti and seeing his personal passion firsthand was incredible. It's not just a business proposition to him or, I gather, the entire staff at Soles4Souls. They all believe in the mission and literally live it, breathe it.

Knowing how many trips David does in a year, it's hard on one's emotions, but I think he exemplified the Soles4Souls mission. Now that we've been and we've seen what Soles4Souls is doing on the ground, we want to share that with our employees.

TAUNA: In the next year, six to ten employees will be able to experience what we have in Haiti. We think that over time, as more people are touched by that experience, the stronger we'll solidify this relationship with Soles4Souls. It made an indelible mark on us, and we think our employees will be no different.

David's commitment and energy and passion, like Patty said, is incredible. He's a true businessman with a heart. There are not a lot of people that are as business savvy and operationally minded, with equal parts compassion, heart, and commitment. That was really important to me, that we have someone who is both professionally savvy and personally committed to our mission and journey with Soles4Souls.

MEANWHILE, DOWN THE COAST ...

Another of S4S's industry partners is headquartered a thousand miles south of Portland, in Los Angeles. As adidas did with performance sports shoes, so did Chinese Laundry make its name catering to a major piece of the footwear market's pie chart: fashion shoes for women.

Now in its second generation, CELS, the brand's parent company, takes its name from its founder's family members: mother Carol, daughters Elyse and Lauren, and son Stewart. Husband and father

Bob Goldman named Stewart the chief operating officer in early 2016.

ANOTHER VOICE

STEWART GOLDMAN
COO, CHINESE LAUNDRY

Ever since I can remember, I've been in the business. Literally. I started driving a forklift—I shouldn't say driving, I should say crashing!—in the warehouse as a child.

I've been through every department of the company. When I stepped over to COO from executive vice president, I already knew about Soles4Souls. We've donated to them throughout the years. I started a dialogue with Buddy about some of the micro-enterprises and the good deeds they were doing.

He mentioned that he was doing a program in Moldova and potentially other programs in Africa. We met a few times at trade shows, had a coffee, and talked about it. I said I'd love to be supportive of it. We went ahead and made a donation, around 550,000 pairs of shoes, which went to Moldova. That was in 2016.

We'd helped with all different kinds of causes and not-for-profits for years. After Hurricane Katrina, we donated hundreds of thousands of pairs of shoes to Operation Blessing.

I like Soles4Souls. Not only are they giving away a pair of shoes that help a person, they're also giving shoes to people to create enterprise. It's the old saying, if you want to help somebody survive, rather than giving them a fish to eat, teach them how to fish. I think it's a great program.

HOW S4S HELPS CHINESE LAUNDRY

As a company, you build up reserves of inventory.

My father believes in "the long tail," meaning all shoes are good. It doesn't matter if it's the end of the season. They come back in style, because style is cyclical. A few years go by and they're wearing wedges again, or they're wearing peep toes or other styles.

We have our own warehousing, so inventories build up. When you've got half a million or a million or two million pairs of shoes in stock and you're running through your inventory levels on current styles, you have to decide: "Do I want to close out goods, liquidate, or donate?"

Sometimes, we look at our market and decide to donate a few hundred thousand pair. Provided they are going to a foreign country, they are going to help people in need and not adversely affect the inventory that flows into your marketplace. We're selling millions of pairs of shoes in the United States, for example. If we donate a million pairs of shoes that stay in the United States, it has an effect.

A perfect example: We did a rebrand last year. We'd been rolling out the new product, and we had great success with the rebranding and new packaging. We had fantastic shoes in inventory that were perfect, but with the old logos. Soles4Souls was a perfect opportunity to donate and help people who need the shoes, and also to clear inventory that otherwise we'd have to repackage.

It's a nice, easy way for a company to move goods, one that both helps people and creates space in the warehouse—without adversely affecting inventory flow in the marketplace.

Soles4Souls made it easy. They said, "These are the markets we can help micro-enterprises in, and these are the markets we can donate shoes in." They were a fantastic solution; not only did they give you the information on where they're going to distribute the goods, but we made all the arrangements through them. The trucks picked up the goods, and Soles4Souls gave us proof of export and proof of where the goods are going. It's one-stop shopping.

Moldova was great for us; we don't have distribution there, so it doesn't affect our marketplace.

But let's say we chose Africa or another area that is in need, that doesn't affect our distribution channels. I think if multiple companies would think like this and get on board, it would help Soles4Souls take care of tens of thousands—if not millions—of people who are in need across the globe, because not every company distributes to the same countries.

By working with different companies, Soles4Souls is able to fill the map, and take care of a need. I think we all want to help people, and Soles4Souls is the hub—they have the ability to facilitate that.

It's a win-win for everybody.

BEYOND BRANDS

We're well on the way to making Stewart's vision a reality. In addition to Chinese Laundry and adidas, Soles4Souls is proud to count literally hundreds of brands familiar to every American household as supporters, among them Allbirds, BCNY, Brighton Collectibles, Brooks, Caleres, CCILU, Chico's, DSW, Forever 21, New Balance, NYDJ, Rockport, Shoes for Crews, Stitch Fix, The North Face, Timberland, Uggs, Wolverine, and Zappos.

We greatly value these relationships. The shoes and apparel S4S secures through the combination of new and gently used donated product is key to furthering our mission.

There's another group of industry partners we value just as much. They may not be household names beyond the communities they serve, but their positive impact on our mission and dedication to it is no less exemplary nor important. They are independent retailers, in cities and towns across the country. A not-for-profit organization and S4S industry partner, the National Shoe Retailers Association, represents them.

Chuck Schuyler is the president of NSRA. Begun in 1912, it advocates on behalf of independent shoe retailers to manufacturers, suppliers, and the broader footwear industry. Chuck first learned of S4S at a national market, a thrice-yearly industry event showcasing the latest in foot apparel.

"The charity was just getting started," Chuck said. "Wayne told me what he was doing and I really liked what I was hearing. It made so much sense. It was such a simple idea—why didn't anyone do that before? You've got a product that's no longer valuable here, but there's millions of people that need it."

Chuck helped get the word out, communicating to NSRA's member database. "We could do that more efficiently and certainly with better cost effectiveness. We started marketing it, and over the next few years, more and more of our members began participating, donating shoes and socks."

In 2011, the relationship fully blossomed.

"We started an annual leadership conference at different cities in the United States. We bring in the top independent footwear retailers and the top vendors that support the independent community. They work together on how to deal with today's challenges. It just made sense, since we had everybody together, to add a charitable component. We turned to Soles4Souls, and that's where our relationship really took off."

S4S and NSRA now partner at each of the association's leadership conferences. Together we distribute shoes at no cost in the host city, prior to each conference's start. The distribution has benefited homeless shelters, schools in disadvantaged neighborhoods, a whole gamut of people in need.

"We were in San Antonio," Chuck said, describing a recent distribution. "In something like two and a half hours, we fit over four hundred kids in shoes. We're always able to bring about 125 to 140 volunteers; we pack them in buses and go to the site, and that's about all the credit we can take. Soles4Souls has already done all the research and the logistics. The shoes are waiting," he said. "As soon as our volunteers hit the ground, we have people moving shoes, people fitting shoes. It's amazing to see, but they're all in the shoe business, so it's just a natural thing, who goes where."

These events' benefits extend beyond the recipients of the brand-new shoes that are distributed.

"We get tremendous exposure through our independent channel, but also to the entire industry, because we market this pretty aggressively. Vendors, retailers, everybody in the footwear industry sees what we're doing."

BOTTOM-LINE BENEFITS

The synergies that accrue to NSRA's member retailers through S4S are manifold. Beyond positive PR and the chance to shed excess inventory, Chuck's members see—and often seize—the unique opportunity for direct customer engagement that S4S provides.

"The marketing programs bring in two pairs of gently used shoes and get this kind of discount; our retailers are extremely creative and come up with plans. They win with more customers coming through the door, and obviously Soles4Souls wins, too," Chuck said.

"I think that's probably where the greatest amount of donations are made, more than through excess inventory. At sponsored events in local communities. Everybody wins, that's the nice thing about this. We don't have records, but if you would take our couple thousand stores, over ten years, I imagine that's a pretty high number of pairs which have been donated, which is really a nice thing. There's no downside on any of it."

The Shoe Mill, in Portland (Patty Goffe of adidas mentioned it earlier in the chapter), is one of NSRA's roughly two thousand member retailers.

Another is a group of fourth-generation stores in greater Milwaukee: Stan's Fit For Your Feet. Their experience with collecting and distributing shoes predates even S4S's founding—by nearly a decade!

ANOTHER VOICE

JIM SADJAK

PRESIDENT AND CEO,
STAN'S FIT FOR YOUR FEET

We call our event "Share a Pair," and it's held every February. When shoe collection came out on more of a national and global level, it made sense for us to share the shoes we were collecting with that global effort.

We do a lot of distribution of shoes to our local community—homeless shelters, women's shelters—over the years we've done a lot of that work. We take our staff for a fitting to a homeless shelter, and my goodness, we have homeless people standing around the corner waiting for shoes. It's very gratifying, and it helps our community.

We go on television and have a lot of public service announcements. We send mailers out to our customer list, and really hype it up. We have so many shoes. Over the years it's been a tremendous amount, and we felt it was really important to share the shoes with Soles4Souls. That overabundance of shoes that we collect—we're so passionate about this as a project for our store that we rent a warehouse.

We collect shoes year-round. It's really gotten to be a major project for our company, for both our family stores—Stan's Fit For Your Feet—and our two New Balance stores.

We've created our own collection boxes. We're known as a place to drop shoes off, and there's not a day that goes by that our collection boxes aren't filled to the brim. People just clean out their closets.

Jim Sadjak at his store in Milwaukee.

It's amazing, the different groups that catch on to this. I just got a call from a group of attorneys, they made it their firm's special community project. We've had Girl Scout and Boy Scout troops collecting shoes for us. We've had grade schools that made it a project. Southwest Airlines has done it locally—I mean, the list goes on and on. People really feel good about this. They know that these gently worn shoes will have a life after their original life.

This past Saturday, in the sleet and rain, we loaded a trailer with 218 cases, a [shipping] container load. About once a year we clean out the warehouse and send the shoes wherever the Soles4Souls crew instructs us to send them. We use our staff, and usually tie in a local high school to help, as a service project.

On Saturday, there were a number of young men from one of the all-boys schools here. It's kind of a win-win. They get their service credits, and they help us do some of the muscle work.

THE "STAN'S" STORY

Grandfather started a store in Milwaukee about 1923, and then after World War II, my dad—Stan—came back and saw a need for all the families that were being created after the war. He started his business in 1950.

This is our sixty-seventh year. I joined after I graduated from college in 1972, and now I'm happy to say that the fourth generation, my four children, have all come into the business. That's been a real blessing. I never thought all four would jump into the business, but they did—and I've got to tell you, this next generation of ours is very into community involvement. I can't tell you how many things they were involved in our stores, and I think that's what local businesses need to do.

The Soles4Souls and our Share a Pair event is certainly a highlight, but we're involved with Children's Hospital and many of the charity races and runs here in the Milwaukee area. We're constantly out there.

Any business in a community I think really needs to look at how they can be involved. It's up to brick-and-mortar stores to make a difference. So much is being said about online businesses today, but that doesn't touch the neighborhood.

If you want to stay relevant in top-of-mind awareness, you've got to make some noise. You've got to show you care about the people you do business with, and the people in your community.

NEW ORLEANS—AND THE BIGGER PICTURE

We did the National Shoe Retailers Association distribution with Soles4Souls down in New Orleans, in 2011.

To see the look on people's faces as they were coming in, homeless people who were displaced, in the terribly devastated districts down there, six years after the storm [Hurricane Katrina].

I remember there was one gentleman that came in. He was in a wheelchair. He did not have any shoes on, and his feet were in awful shape. He had some open sores, and no one wanted to work with him.

And I remember my daughter, who was probably twenty-five at the time, she was along on the trip, gloved up, while people were saying, "Ooh, I don't want to get into that." I was so proud of Megan. She just got in there, and she said, "I'm going to take care of this guy, because everybody is just kind of standing around and looking."

She measured him, and we got him some shoes, and she put his socks on. And I was just so proud of her for getting involved, not being afraid to roll up her sleeves and take care of this guy.

This next generation, these millennials, are a group in time that's about giving. It's important for them to give back. Megan and her brother, Ben, went on a Soles4Souls trip to Guatemala. It was life-changing. Life-changing; just an unbelievable experience.

It's those kinds of things that make a difference. Not just collecting shoes for micro-enterprises. The ripple effect of this program is dynamic. It's encouraged us to do more things locally, it's gotten retailers to come together that in some cases could be competitors. To kneel down on the floor and take care of five hundred kids. It's given many people the opportunity to travel around the world for distributions.

I think we need to look at that bigger picture.

Jim is not alone in recognizing the many positive effects of the work Soles4Souls pursues.

Those effects touch all who help us, and those we serve. They testify to the profound power of the idea that struck Wayne Elsey as he watched the devastation of the Indian Ocean tsunami unfold in 2004.

But Soles4Souls didn't have to survive. Just because we believed we were doing good didn't give us some special right to exist. As discussed earlier, luck is always a factor, and we did have some lucky breaks. But we also made some very conscious decisions to do things differently.

Those changes are what the final chapter is about.

CHAPTER 9

A NEW TWIST ON T.E.A.M.

I sincerely thank everyone who lent their voices to telling the story of S4S's impact on their countries, cities, neighborhoods, organizations, and their own lives. Their unwavering belief in our mission of Wearing Out Poverty has taken it from the stuff of dreams to producing tangible results for real people.

That's a big deal for any organization, but for one that nearly folded its tent not so long ago, it borders on the miraculous. I'd like to share how the efforts we made to do things differently allowed Soles4Souls to survive its darker days, and allowed us to evolve into the thriving, mission-driven organization it has become.

Kelly Modena was particularly affected by that journey.

"WHAT AM I DOING?"

We first met Kelly, now S4S's director of community partnerships, in chapter 7. She joined the organization in 2011.

Kelly left a lucrative sales job for one she believed could change people's lives for the better. But when, like the rest of the staff, she awoke one Sunday morning to front-page stories questioning S4S's governance and financial dealings under its founder, Kelly was stunned. One report said the organization was selling shoes that had been donated for disaster relief.

Kelly distributing shoes in Nashville.

"I remember a lot of our team asking, 'Are we selling our shoes? What does that mean? What does that look like? Are we doing something good, or is this bad?'" Kelly remembered. "It sent us all into kind of a tailspin, because we didn't really know."

She sat down with David Graben, Soles4Souls' then-executive vice president, now chief operating officer.

"I just said, 'What am I doing? Tell me what I'm really doing here. Where are our shoes going?'" Kelly said, recalling her confusion. "As an organization, we really weren't talking a lot about micro-enterprise. I knew we were doing some of that indirectly, but we definitely weren't developing our direct micro at that time.

"David and I had a candid conversation. He showed me a ton of pictures of where he had been and who he had seen, information I could then take to my volunteers. I was astonished. I wondered, why was that ever hidden? We should be shouting from the mountains that we're doing this! This is so cool!"

Kelly found that telling the story amid the media scrutiny was no picnic. "When we first started talking about micro-enterprise I fumbled, because it had been this big thing [in the newspaper]. It was like the elephant in the room that nobody knew how to explain, when really, what we were doing was so amazing. But once [Buddy] got here, set the tone, and started sharing [his] stories, it was easier. Not all of us travel like [him] and David and our travel team, but once [Buddy] introduced the T.E.A.M. concept, it changed everything."

Kelly is referring to an internal dialogue begun at my urging, soon after I was hired. We started talking about our values, what mattered to us as we did our work—the "why" behind the shoes. We didn't set out to come up with an acronym—they can be so cheesy—but we wound up with one: T.E.A.M.

And it was spot on because, given what I walked into as S4S's new CEO, it was clear it was going to take all of us to get things back on track.

ANOTHER VOICE

NELSON WILSON
FORMER S4S BOARD MEMBER

When Wayne [Elsey] resigned, we were bleeding money like crazy. It was awful.

So there we were, with no CEO. We had some employees who were instrumental in holding the organization together, but David Graben was the glue during the transition to Buddy.

Our main goal was to stop the bleeding, stabilize the office, and then hire a CEO. We hired the Center for Not-for-Profit Management here in Nashville, who did a nationwide search that generated more than one hundred candidates. After a months-long process, we finally got it down to three final candidates, and Buddy was one of those. Buddy had long hair. [*Buddy here. I still do, and it's a fact the closely-cropped Nelson never misses a chance to point out!*]

We brought the candidates to Nashville to meet with the board. People talked about what they could do for the charity and shared their work experience with us. Buddy's resume stood out. He thought it would be exciting to be part of something that gives people a chance to improve their lives, and to do it with shoes. His answers just resonated with, "I want to help people, and I see this as a way of helping people."

That's why Buddy was chosen. You could see his heart was helping others. He could see the potential for doing that, through all the mess and the muck that was going on. He brought in a CFO [Les Ward] and they cleaned up the financials, got us out of the lawsuits, and started focusing on micro-enterprise. Suddenly, with the transparency that he brought, shoe companies started coming back.

We were so close to shutting the doors. It's unbelievable.

Paul, my brother, and I—our attitudes are that God put Buddy in this situation at that time because, of all the candidates on that list, we do not think Soles4Souls would be in business had it not been for Buddy. He took to heart the little bit of micro-enterprise that we started and has made it into a worldwide vision.

His number-one thing when he came in was transparency. He got it to the point where people began to trust us again, and here we are today.

As you've probably guessed, the "T" in the T.E.A.M acronym we created at Soles4Souls stands for **Transparent.**

Its other attributes—**Entrepreneurial, Accountable,** and **Meaningful**—help us function efficiently and effectively each day, without losing sight of who we are here for. But if S4S's brush with death proved nothing else, it's the absolute necessity of complete transparency in all we do.

A favorite quote of mine is from one of the most successful businesspeople of all time, Warren Buffet: "It takes twenty years to build a reputation and five minutes to ruin it. If you think about that, you'll do things differently."

It took Soles4Souls much less than twenty years to build its reputation for doing good, by distributing shoes to those affected by two of human history's worst natural disasters. It quickly became clear to me that our only hope for climbing out of the ditch we were in, with our reputation in question, lay in creating a new, unambiguous level of transparency.

People rightly believe charitable organizations are created to do good. But when *any* organization—not-for-profit, for-profit, governmental—is thought to be acting in ways that contradict its mission or that may be harmful to others, people quickly lose trust.

This is true even when the perception is false, as was the case with S4S's early work in micro-enterprise. The real problem was not that S4S was selling donated shoes. The real problem was the organization's failure to explain *why* and *how*. That led people to conclude that something was shady, and once that perception takes hold, it is very hard to shake.

Complete transparency is the only answer. It is not only the surest way to win the trust of everyone with a stake in the organization, but is also the great *protector* of that trust. When an organization openly documents what it is doing and shares the reasons why, it is also asking potential stakeholders a question: "Are you with us?" Conversely, an inability, reluctance, or outright refusal to share actions and rationale prompts prospective allies to ask a very different question: "What are you hiding?"

Soles4Souls began its life distributing new shoes at no cost to people in need, and it bears repeating: we will never stop doing so. It was therefore critical that we address the legitimate concerns which had been raised among our stakeholders.

Collectors of gently used product—volunteers like Michele James and Claire Baker and Karin Leaver—have seen the positive effects of *both* free distribution and micro-enterprise firsthand. They needed little convincing when Soles4Souls embraced its broader mission. But our industry partners lacked such confirmation, so some, understandably, were less sure.

JIM SADJAK, STAN'S FIT FOR YOUR FEET:

"We never lost sight of the mission. There were some rocky times, [but] I still knew that people were being helped. Micro-enterprise is used by a lot of organizations; I think the tough part was that it was not explained well.

"Now that Buddy has come in and has been very open about it, I think people are saying, 'Yeah, that makes sense.' Buddy righted the ship, and that has helped pull the status of Soles4Souls up to another level. As long as they continue to be open and honest and to communicate, I see nothing but good things."

PATTY GOFFE, ADIDAS:

"There was a little rough patch there, but I think David [Graben] handled the whole transition very diplomatically and reassuringly. Even though there was a lot going on in the background, I'm sure, on the Soles4Souls side, it was not all that apparent.

"David was great in addressing them and reassuring me that nothing was going to really change in terms of their support of our partnership and what they were doing with our product. So I would definitely credit him with a smooth transition during a time of a lot of questions and insecurity. He handled it really well."

CHUCK SCHUYLER, NSRA:

"Without the integrity of the organization, the caring and the passionate people that are [at Soles4Souls]—Buddy, David, Pattie, and Tiffany are the quick four names we've worked with for years that come to mind—I don't think the success would have been anywhere close to what they're enjoying today. People make everything work. That's why Soles4Souls is so successful and helps so many people."

STEWART GOLDMAN, CHINESE LAUNDRY:

"There are so many worthwhile charities, and they're all valuable and important. At the end of the day, for us, Soles4Souls has been very easy to work with and legitimate.

"You hear these horror stories where a company takes donations and doesn't do what they're supposed to do with it. With Soles4Souls, you can see the effects of what they do. They'll show you the videos of when they're working with people, making donations and/or setting up micro-enterprises, which develop opportunities for people that they wouldn't otherwise have."

As I look back over Soles4Souls' first decade or so and my time as CEO, it's amazing that we're here. The story could have been one of opportunity missed, potential not realized, lives not transformed.

Instead, as you've heard from so many different people, and in spite of the missteps, we're alive and well. Thirty million pairs of shoes and millions of pounds of clothing later, we're on track to have $500 million of economic impact by 2020.

It hits me again and again that while it didn't have to be this way, it is. Because of individuals and companies who believed in a better way to use their time, money, and product, millions of people in the United States and around the world will have healthier lives and better livelihoods. When I say ,"We did that," I really mean the biggest "we" imaginable.

From a sixteen-year-old girl to a seventy-one-year-old retiree, they made this possible.

From one of the largest global athletic brands to an independent retailer in Milwaukee, they made this possible.

The team and board of Soles4Souls, who had the courage to continue on—they made this possible.

To paraphrase Lao Tzu, "Leadership is best when people barely know it exists, when the work is done, the aim fulfilled, and the people say: we did it ourselves."

At Soles4Souls, I believe that sense has never been felt more strongly than it is right now.

We believe Wearing Out Poverty is a world-changing idea. We are seeing the positive results of that effort. I hope that after reading the stories of all those involved (our direct partners, the entrepreneurs, the collectors, and industry partners), you see it as well. With a strong foundation now in place, we're set to scale up our model for even greater impact for more people. We hope to add your voice to that story soon!

will you walk with us?

Whether you are interested in furthering Soles4Souls' mission as a shoe collector, industry partner, in-country partner, a traveler, or in some other capacity, we'd like to hear from you.

Maybe this book has prompted an idea we've not yet considered. We'd like to hear it.

Perhaps you'd like to make a small (or large!) donation. Whether it's unrestricted or one with strings attached—shoestrings—give us a call, send us an email, or find a drop-off location near you.

Our website provides resources you'll need to get started, no matter how you'd like to help.

www.soles4souls.org

THANK YOU IN ADVANCE FOR VISITING, AND THANKS FOR READING.
FROM ALL OF US.